Learning
Experiences
in Educational
Psychology

Learning Experiences in Educational Psychology

Robert L. Morasky

State University of New York
at Plattsburgh

WM. C. BROWN COMPANY PUBLISHERS
Dubuque, Iowa

Contents

Preface   vii

Introduction   ix

UNIT **1**   Personality and Learning   1

UNIT **2**   Intelligence   31

UNIT **3**   Social Perception   57

UNIT **4**   Conceptual Processes   111

UNIT **5**   Learning   171

UNIT **6**   Teacher-Student Interaction   193

UNIT **7**   Behavior Management   209

UNIT **8**   Information Theory—Feedback   239

UNIT **9**   Instructional Design   265

Preface

It is important that the reader of this book understands clearly the purpose of the unusual format since the innovative design of the book makes it a rarity among college texts. A notion basic to the design of this book is that concrete, realistic experiences are an essential aspect of meaningful learning; therefore, the author has provided the material and structure for experiences to accompany each different topic in the book. Each topic or unit consists of a short introduction, a description of the experience, a checklist for the student to follow and the materials necessary to complete, evaluate, and report on the experience. Following each experience are suggested additional activities and readings for the reader who is interested in pursuing the topic.

Another way of looking at each unit topic is that the reader will not discover what information psychologists *know* who emphasize that topic, but, rather, what psychologists *do* with that approach. For instance, ask yourself, What do psychologists do who emphasize intelligence and place a great deal of importance on it as an approach to educational problems? Among other things, they try to define intelligence, make up instruments for measuring intelligence, and administer intelligence tests. That is precisely what the reader is given the opportunity to do in Unit Two. In addition, references are provided at the end of each unit for the reader who wishes to "know" what another psychologist "knows."

The major theme running through the units can be described as moving from emphasis on the student and his characteristics in Units One, Two, Three, Four and Five to the student and the teacher and their influence over each other in Units Six, Seven, Eight and Nine. In that portion of the book which deals with the student, individual differences are emphasized through the topics, personality, intelligence, social perception, conceptual processes and learning. Topics such as interaction analysis, behavior management, information feedback, and instructional design provide impetus for consideration of the student and teacher as reciprocal influences.

The laboratory for the experiences in this book can be a college dormitory room, a seminar class, a kitchen table, or any other environment which is a part of the reader's everyday life. The subjects in the experiences can be roommates, girlfriends, classmates, a husband or wife or any other individual who is most relevant to the reader and to the task at hand. This involvement with activities and people rather than information and books tends to generate interest and curiosity on the part of the reader. "Book learning" will come about eventually, but it will be the result of personal interest instead of avoidance of poor grades.

This book differs from the other workbooks or lab manuals in another important way. The author is not trying to convince the reader of the particular value of the approaches given. The experiences are not completely cut-and-dried. It is not always predictable what the results will be; but be assured that there will be results, and that they can be reported—but the reader is encouraged to enjoy the freedom of observing and reporting fresh and, perhaps, peculiar results. For example, who can predict how a roommate will respond to a personality assessment scale after returning home from an enjoyable evening at the local campus gathering place, or how a class will respond to a teacher who refuses to give in to student silence when a question is presented? The variables possibly influencing the results of each experience are as important for the reader to observe and report as the results themselves.

Obviously, this book was planned for prospective teachers or practicing teachers who wish to find what psychology has to offer education. On the other hand, it should not be assumed that only education majors would benefit from the experiences in this book.

It must be said that Unit Seven, Behavior Management, could not have been developed without the instruction, support, criticism and work of my colleague, Dr. James M. Johnson. Unit Seven is truly his accomplishment much more than mine. To say that we are coauthors of that section is to say that he wrote it and I edited and inserted it in the book.

The author must also acknowledge the tremendous contributions Dr. Donald E. P. Smith of the University of Michigan made to the philosophy behind the design of this book. Many psychologists understand learning, but few can help others achieve a degree of understanding as Dr. Smith has done. In addition, the author would surely be remiss if he did not acknowledge the hundreds of students at the State University College at Plattsburgh, whose criticisms, patience, and encouragement made this book possible.

Introduction

There is a belief among some psychologists that a course in educational psychology can be taught as well with an introductory or general psychology textbook as with a specialized book on educational psychology. The reasoning behind this belief seems to be that the domain of educational psychology is *all* psychological information. That is, whatever any psychologist knows about human behavior is fair game for educational psychology as long as it has some application to education. Therefore, a general text will provide as well as any book the basic information or principles the student will have to apply when the status of "teacher" is attained. The belief in a sense is well-founded. The domain of psychology is the study of man's behavior and its ramifications; the domain of educational psychology is to apply what we know about man and his behavior to the educational process.

An attempt has been made in this book to present several different approaches which psychologists have taken to solve problems related to the educational process in the United States. The approaches differ markedly in philosophy and method. *The reader should not assume that every approach is perfect and immune to attack.* Do not assume that the author would defend each approach with his life! On the contrary, the author encourages the reader to critically analyze and compare the various approaches. In some cases, the approaches are complementary, and the reader can consider adopting parts or all of different approaches. In other cases, the approaches are incompatible with each other and, in fact, contradictory. *It is the hope of the author that the reader will become sufficiently knowledgeable so as to make choices and begin to coordinate those approaches which seem to be most acceptable.*

This book does not cover every approach that a psychologist could possibly take to education, nor is it an attempt to condense a multitude of facts and theories into one volume. It is instead a sample of nine psychological approaches to learning and teaching which will provide a wide and varied coverage of educational psychology. Basically, educational psychology is viewed by the author as a discipline in which psychologists study problems of education and learning. The individual units in this book present a few problems and some of the different ways psychologists have approached these problems. For example, Unit Two, Intelligence, is simply *an example* of one approach, and the other units are likewise representative of other approaches.

Several things appear in this book which are not normally found in books, but which were included in order to facilitate the experience and, hence, the learning of the reader. The *Background* information at the beginning of each unit is simply an introduction to the topic. There are very few facts or theories apparent in the background sections. When reading the Background, do so with the knowledge that the information will subsequently be used to better comprehend and evaluate the activity associated with that topic. The activity or *Experience* portion of each unit is introduced by statements called *Experience Objectives* which state what should be done. In order to help sequence the various components of the Experiences, *Suggested Procedures* are presented immediately after the Experience Objectives. The detailed, step by step procedures do not imply that readers are ignoramuses who can't find or design worthwhile experiences, but rather, that structure sometimes insures more productive responses. In the early stages of the development of this book, the author discovered that many readers welcomed the structure provided by the Suggested Procedures, and asked that *Checklists* also be included so that step by step progress could be demonstrated. The reader may wish to use the checklists, and if so, they are there for his convenience.

Following the Experience materials are unit *Summaries*. The Summary is an important aspect of each unit because it includes more than just a review of what came before it. The one important item which comes before each Summary is the Experience, and there is no simple way of reviewing it, but questions do provide a means of evaluating it. So the Summary of each unit is loaded with questions (and sometimes loaded questions). The reader will want to consider each question in light of the Experience. While reading the Summary, the reader may discover that much more was learned from the Experience than was initially apparent.

If the reader wishes to extend his work and learning about a topic, the *Suggested Additional Activities* provide semi-structured designs for added experiences. Those people who choose to engage in additional Experiences can free-lance a bit and begin their own preplanned experiential learning.

The Experience and the Suggested Additional Activities often stimulate sufficient interest for the reader to want some facts and theories about the topic, and the *Suggested Additional Readings* lists provide the necessary references. Generally, the Readings lists are divided into three sub-lists; those which provide general information, those which provide more detailed information, and those which concentrate on detailed, specific aspects of the topic. The journal references are in most cases limited to four or five well-known periodicals which can be found in most college libraries.

Extensive use of questions is made in the book. Questions seem to play an important role in learning. For example, questions are a vital part of programmed instruction. Rothkopf[1] has demonstrated the positive effect of questions on learning from written material, and Robinson[2] made questions a major component in the SQ4R reading technique. Therefore, it seems reasonable that an author provide questions which the reader can use as study or reading aids. It is also hoped that the reader will use the questions provided initially as a source of uncertainty—a reason for reading the text. Secondly, the reader can use the questions for review purposes. Thirdly, questions in the text provide a quick indexing scheme when the reader has generated his own question. Finally, questions provide a means of final self-evaluation for the reader who is willing to ask himself the question, Do I know the answer to that question?

1. E. Z. Rothkopf, "Some Theoretical and Experimental Approaches to Problems in Written Instruction," In J. D. Krumboltz ed. *Learning and the Educational Process* (Chicago: Rand McNally, 1965).
2. F. P. Robinson "Effective Study" (New York: Harper and Row, 1970).

UNIT 1

Personality and Learning

♦ BACKGROUND

Most teachers are concerned at sometime or another with individual differences in children. The teaching profession abounds with cliches such as:

A teacher must consider the whole child. It is not sufficient to consider only one characteristic.

Teachers must take into account the personality of each student, and regard each one as an individual.

Children do not learn in the same way. Just as personalities differ, so also do modes of learning differ.

Teachers who take these statements as principles and attempt to apply them to actual classroom practice must begin to consider the role of personality in individual differences. Immediately, the questions arise, What is personality? or How do personalities differ from child to child? or How do differences in personality relate to differences in classroom practice? Psychologists also consider these questions, and the answers arrived at by psychologists can help the classroom teacher. In this Unit we will look at one way in which psychologists work with personality. In addition you will be given the opportunity to use one of the tools employed by psychologists to measure personality and relate that measurement to learning. We will begin, however, by examining some background information about personality.

1

What does a psychologist mean when he uses the term, "personality"?

At the beginning of a discussion like this it must be stressed that psychology as a discipline does not consist of a catalog of indisputable facts. Therefore, not all psychologists view all things alike. So, not all psychologists will agree to one definition of personality. One very prominent psychologist described personality as "the dynamic organization within the individual of those psychophysical systems that determine his unique adjustments to his environment." It is reasonable to assume that such a definition helps the psychologist, but does it help the teacher? Consider, for example, a student, Johnny, who responds better to nondirected activities than Jerry. Johnny's teacher might infer that Johnny's performance is related to his personality. A psychologist might infer that the same performance is related to the dynamic organization of Johnny's psychophysical systems. Both inferences relate to the performance, but neither provides the teacher with information to apply to classroom practice. Perhaps, the psychologist's definition of personality is not as important as his ideas about the structure of personality.

What does the psychologist mean by "personality structure"?

Personality is viewed by some psychologists as consisting of several parts or components. These components are called *behavior traits*. A person's total personality or his personality structure would be at least the sum of the various behavior traits, if not also the effect of the interaction between the traits.

Let us consider a trait we will label "cheerfulness." Given that trait, it is possible to assess with more or less accuracy the degree to which any individual possesses that trait. For instance, subjective evaluation of a student by a teacher might result in the statement, "He certainly has a cheerful personality." A more definite statement would be, "My evaluation ranks him high on the trait, cheerfulness." This latter statement implies that the trait, cheerfulness, is of a continuous nature, from high to low, and this is usually true of behavior traits identified by psychologists. Some behavior traits are listed below. How would you subjectively rate yourself on each one?

Low ——————— INDEPENDENCE ——————— High

Low ——————— ANXIETY ——————— High

Low ——————— SERIOUSNESS ——————— High

Low ——————— RELIABILITY ——————— High

Note that each of the traits shown above is placed on a continuum, and extends from low to high. In addition each is representative of some class of observable behaviors. For example, if a person consistently delivers books to you when he says he will, you usually describe him as "reliable." He would probably be ranked at the high end of the "reliability" continuum. This does not mean that reliability is like skin and that he has it. Rather, what we are saying is that there are degrees of reliability, and theoretically, each individual exhibits only so much of any trait. It, therefore, becomes possible to say that people differ according to the degree to which they exhibit various behavior traits. Individual differences, therefore, can be described as differences in behavior traits rather than just differences in "personality." The next question faced by the psychologist is, How do I measure the degree to which someone possesses a trait?

How are behavior traits measured?

Behavior traits could be assessed by direct observation of the individual. For example, suppose we are measuring "authoritarianism" and use as a measure the number of commands to someone else a person makes each day. Direct observation methods would require that the psychologist follow the person around and count the number of times commands were given. This method, for obvious reasons, is usually not practical. Consider the problem of trying to record and evaluate someone's behavior for an extended period, say, a month or two!

On the other hand, if behavior traits are consistent and stable within individuals, they should be evident even in a standardized situation. It is on this basis that psychologists have developed tests for assessing various behavior traits. For example, a series of questions about whether one would rather go somewhere alone or with friends might be a valid measure for the behavior trait, "independence." A high score on such a test could indicate that the person possessed the behavior trait, "independence," to a high degree. From a series of assessment tests, it is possible to develop a profile, consisting of several rankings on several different traits.

With this information it is possible for the psychologist and the teacher to talk about specific differences in "personality." But, so what? How would that information help a teacher?

How are behavior trait differences related to education?

Once the psychologist has broken personality down into specific behavior traits, and developed what he believes is a tool for measuring the traits, he can investigate differences in reading, memorizing, writing, and other skills based on trait differences. For example, suppose the psychologist identifies "independence" as a behavior trait and develops a questionnaire for measuring that trait. After giving the questionnaire to a group of subjects, he can rank them along the continuum from "high independence" to "low independence." Suppose, then, that he discovers that the subjects with "high independence" rankings also consistently learn more from mediated materials than do "low independence" people. The psychologist can, then, help the teacher identify and predict who will benefit most from a film, and who should, perhaps, receive additional and personal help.

By following a strategy such as the one described above, the psychologist can assess the behavior traits of students at various levels and relate them to specific aspects of the educational process.

◆ AN EXPERIENCE

You now have enough background to meaningfully profit from performing some of the behaviors which a psychologist might perform who is concerned with personality differences and learning. In the experience which follows, you should look critically at the measurement tool used, its practicality, its validity, and above all, your influence on its usefulness. Environmental or situational variables can influence the scores obtained. Be sure to watch for these factors. All the materials you need to complete the experience can be found on the next several pages. The main things you should do in this experience are called *Experience Objectives*. They are listed below.

Experience Objectives

1. You should prepare four test questions which will become items 37, 38, 39, and 40 of the Simulated Personality Assessment Scale (SPAS).
2. You should administer and score the Simulated Personality Assessment Scale (SPAS). (The subject can be another college student.)
3. You should read and interpret the results from the SPAS to the subject in Experience Objective 1 above. (The SPAS Test Manual has written descriptions corresponding to various test scores. You may read the appropriate description to your subject directly from the manual.)
4. You should interview the subject from Experience Objective 1 immediately after reading the test interpretation. (For the format of the interview, see SPAS Interview Guidelines Sheet.)

Suggested Procedure for Achieving the Experience Objectives

1. Read the SPAS Manual, be sure you know the answers to the questions, and take the SPAS yourself. Remember, do not write on the answer sheet or test booklet—you only have one.
2. Write four test items which you feel will discriminate "aggressive" from "nonaggressive" people. Remember the items must be statements which the subject feels is true (for him) or false (for him). Insert the four items in place of questions 37, 38, 39 and 40.
3. Find a subject and administer the SPAS.
4. Interpret the results and read the appropriate description to your subject.
5. Immediately after interpreting his scores to the subject, ask him the questions on the SPAS Interview Guidelines Sheet.
6. Write a description of a proposed teaching strategy you would use with

the SPAS subject. Use the Teaching Strategy Sample as a model and the Strategy Checklist as a guide.

7. Submit the interpretation and the teaching strategy description to an instructor for evaluation.

Progress Chart

Activity	Check each space when completed.
1. Read SPAS manual and test	_____
2. Prepare four test items	_____
3. Administer and score SPAS	_____
4. Read interpretation	_____
5. Interview subject	_____
6. Write Teaching Strategy Description	_____

Simulated Personality Assessment Scale (SPAS) Test Manual

Describe the SPAS.

The SPAS is a thirty-six item questionnaire for measuring two dimensions of personality, aggression and indecision. The SPAS was specially prepared for student use with *Learning Experiences in Educational Psychology.* It is for this reason that it is called a "simulated" assessment scale. Personality assessment scales which are commonly used for clinical and diagnostic purposes by qualified, professional psychologists are typically not available for public distribution, therefore, the SPAS was prepared as a simulation or near approximation to standardized assessment instruments. It was designed to be used with adult students. The SPAS is easily completed, quickly scored, and readily interpreted. The subject's scores on the two dimensions and the meanings of the scores can (and should) be interpreted for the subject.

Give a definition for the dimension "aggression."

Aggression is defined within the context of the SPAS to mean the tendency of a subject to behaviorally exert himself in a situation. Similar to extroversion, aggression implies the outward or overt rather than the inward or covert directing of emotions, values, desires, etc.

Define what is meant by the dimension "indecision."

For the purposes of the SPAS, indecision is defined as the degree to which one is incapable of choosing between alternatives. Low levels of indecision result in rapid and consistent choice-making behavior with little conflict or anxiety, whereas high levels of indecision imply avoidance or delay in the act of choice-making with concurrent conflict and anxiety. "Indecision" is the contrary to "decision"; that is, the SPAS measures the degree to which someone is "not-decisive," rather than the degree to which he is "decisive." The negative dimension is used because of the SPAS scoring procedure which gives the examiner a direct "indecision" value but would require a further manipulation of scores in order to obtain a "decision" value.

How is the SPAS administered?

The SPAS can be given to a group or to individuals. Each subject should be given a copy of the Test Booklet which contains the thirty-six questions and an Answer Sheet on which he will make his responses. The examiner should read the directions at the top of the first page of the test booklet aloud while the subject reads them to himself. *No other information is necessary or should be given.* If subjects ask questions, the examiner should reread the directions which are appropriate to the question posed. Emphasize the point that every item must be answered.

Of course, before the subject is even to the test-taking stage, you must give him some information regarding the nature of the task in order to induce him to volunteer to take the SPAS. You should make it reasonably clear that:

1. The results will be confidential.
2. The results can be discussed by the subject and the examiner and used for counseling purposes.
3. The major benefit to the subject may be an increase in self-knowledge.

How is the SPAS scored?

The examiner should derive two scores from the SPAS. The first score is the indecision dimension score. This is done simply by counting the number of questions which were answered by the "?" choice. It is assumed that this is a direct measure of decision-making behavior, since the subject is given a situation and two choices from which he must choose one or choose the "?." The greater the number of "?" chosen, the greater the degree of indecision. This score will fall somewhere between 0 and 36.

The mean of the test population was 6.5. If we take an actual example, suppose a subject named Sam marked twelve "?," then on the scale in Figure 1.1, a dot would be placed at 12.

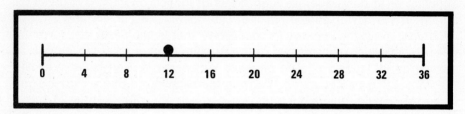

Figure 1.1 An example of a single scale with a subject's score indicated by a dot at 12.

It is easy to see that Sam scored above the mean, but we have yet another score to derive before we can fully utilize the results of the SPAS. To score the aggression dimension, place the SPAS Hand Scoring Stencil (with the proper holes punched out) over the subject's answer sheet making certain that the right edges match. Count the number of X's exposed through the holes. This is the subject's aggression score. We could place the aggression score on a separate scale like the indecision score, but it might be more useful to combine the scores somehow to obtain a composite picture of the two dimensions measured. This is done by using Figure 1.2 in which the aggression scale is placed vertically over the indecision scale and at right angles to it. You can see from Figure 1.2 that the aggression scale intersects the indecision scale at the mean, 6.5. On the other hand, the indecision scale intersects the aggression scale at the mean, 16.5. Once the aggression score is obtained from the subject's answer sheet the examiner should locate the point on the aggression scale where the score falls.

The following procedure is used to combine the scores: First, extend a *vertical* line from the point on the indecision scale where the subject's score falls, second, extend a *horizontal* line from the point on the aggression scale where the subject's score falls. If these two extended lines are perpendicular to their corresponding scales, they will intersect at a point in one of the four quadrants formed by making the two original scales, indecision and aggression, intersect each other at right angles. The four quadrants or sectors are labeled as Group A, B, C, and D. The people whose scores fall in these different quadrants or groups supposedly have different characteristics which can be described. Referring back to the example of Sam who had an indecision score of 12, let us assume he had an aggression score of 21. The lines extended from these two scores inter-

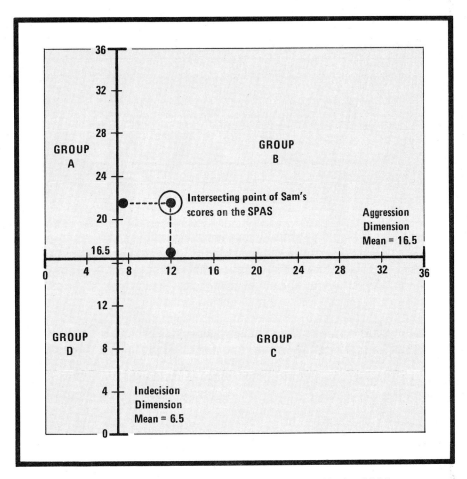

Figure 1.2 A two dimensional scale used with the SPAS.

sect in quadrant B, or as the examiner will tell him, his scores indicate that he will tend to have characteristics common to Group B people. The dotted lines on Figure 1.2 illustrate where Sam's scores intersect.

Describe the characteristics of the persons in the four groups.

The following characteristics are generally true of the subjects who place in particular groups. It should not be assumed that all subjects will behave according to the characteristics listed. That is, some people could achieve scores which would place them in Group A but could, in reality, behave as Group B, C, or D persons. It can be assumed that subjects who score near the dividing lines between groups are less likely to assume the characteristics of a group than those subjects whose scores place them at the extremes of the two continuums.

Group A: Those people whose aggression scores fall between 16.5 and 36, and whose indecision scores fall below 6.5, are in Group A. According to the two dimensions measured, Group A people are high aggression —low indecision. Group A people tend to enter into relationships and associations with more vigor and commitment than people from the other three groups. They tend to be more active in their participation within groups, relationships, and activities. Being reasonably assured that their choice is correct, Group A people tend to respond overtly to aversive situations.

In scholastic matters, Group A people tend to prefer subjects or topics in the Social Sciences much more than those in the Humanities or Sciences, the latter two being somewhat equally low in preference. They much prefer to engage a teacher or other students in discussions than to listen to lectures. Self-directed work is not as preferable as discussions but preferred over lectures. Application of information tends to be of much more concern than theoretical issues to Group A people. In spite of their lack of interest in paper-writing, Group A people tend to select topics quickly and progress readily toward completion of projects. They much prefer multiple-choice-type questions over either true-false or completion-type. They also tend to prefer essay-type questions over true-false and completion-type. In terms of performance on tests, Group A people do almost as well with essay tests as with multiple choice but perform poorly on true-false and completion-type questions tests. Certain subjects within the Group A classification tend to experience rather extreme anxiety over exams while, generally, the group can be said to experience moderate anxiety over exam-taking. Unlike the other groups, a certain number of Group A people tend to experience practically no anxiety over exams.

Group B: Those people whose aggression scores fall between 16.5 and 36, and whose indecision scores fall above 6.5, are in Group B. Descriptively, they would be considered high aggression—high indecision. Generally, such a combination would imply a tendency to exert oneself behaviorally while also exhibiting an inability to make choices between alternatives. Group B people would tend to enter into relationships or activities with a certain amount of forcefulness but without the commitment characteristic of the Group A subjects. They tend to be slow in choosing between various activities and might find themselves actively participating with more than one group. This inability to chose between alternatives, combined with a high level of participation, could lead to awkward situations; for example, participating actively with groups which oppose each other. Aversive situations tend to influence Group B people to redirect their activities.

Scholastically, Group B people tend to prefer either the Sciences or the Social Sciences over the Humanities. There seems to be little difference between their preferences for subjects in Sciences and Social Sciences. They do not prefer to work with a teacher who uses lecture as a primary teaching method but are equally at ease with either discussions or self-directed work. Unlike any of the other groups, Group B people tend to be as much concerned with theoretical issues in classroom work as with practical application of the information. Coinciding with this concern for theory is their preference for laboratory or discussion sessions over lecture presentations. In addition, Group B people tend to enjoy the combination of laboratory and reading assignments which provide both practical application and theoretical experience. Group B people will probably spend more energy on a variety of activities rather than concentrating heavily on the initial project selected. Guidance in the selection of a project will tend to promote more concentrated work in one area. Group B people will not tend to be as independent as either Group A or Group D people. Perhaps because of their interest in theoretical issues, Group B people tend to prefer essay examinations over all other types with a second preference for multiple-choice question exams. In conjunction with this, Group B people tend to perform better on essay question examinations. They do not tend to perform well nor prefer true-false or completion-type question exams. Very few Group B people suffer severe anxiety over exams, and most tend to experience only mild to moderate worries over taking an exam.

Group C: Those people whose aggression scores fall below 16.5 and whose indecision scores are above 6.5, are in Group C. Group C people can be described as having low aggression—high indecision. They tend to be slow about entering into relationships, groups, or activities. Initial attempts at participation are likely to be tentative and without vigor or commitment. They are quick to change affiliations or activities and do not contribute a great deal to any group activity. Participation in *any* group is likely to be more of a problem than participation in too many groups. These people tend to appear as if they ''don't care'' and are avoiding many problems, situations, topics, etc. Because avoidance is not always possible, Group C people tend to be generally more anxious about their activities than do any of the other groups. Aversive conditions do not influence a change in choices but, rather, a change or movement to limbo, or no positive position at all.

In scholastic matters, Group C people prefer the Humanities over either the Sciences or the Social Sciences. Although neither Science nor Social Science offers much appeal to Group C people, they do tend to balance their secondary preferences between these two. Group C people do not dislike lectures as much as Group A and B people, but self-directed work and discussion are about equally preferred over lecture. They seem equally at ease in either lectures or laboratories, but rambling, non-stress discussions are preferred. Both reading assignments and laboratory projects are preferable to term papers. Much like Group A people, Group C people tend to overwhelmingly prefer practical application of information over theoretical issues. Although Group C people tend to prefer multiple-choice questions over all other types, they tend to perform better given essay question tests. A major contributing factor in this regard is probably their lack of skill in choosing quickly and correctly. A majority of Group C people tend to experience from moderate to severe anxiety about test situations. Very few seem to experience no anxiety over exams. Teacher guidance is almost necessary in order to stimulate a moderate level of directed, purposeful behavior.

Group D: Those people whose aggression scores fall below 16.5, and whose indecision scores fall below 6.5, are in Group D. Dimensionally, these people are low aggression—low indecision. Group D people tend to make up their minds rather rapidly, and making choices is not usually a problem. They are not likely to act upon their decisions, however. Although they are fairly certain about their choices, Group D people are not likely to persist in defending decisions. Like the Group C people, Group D people tend not to enter into relationships quickly or with much vigor. However, once a relationship has been established, a group joined, or an activity selected, this group tends to stick with the choice. Participation will not usually be extensive. These people tend to be viewed as loyal, but passive. To a point aversive conditions tend to have little effect on their behavior or lack of it.

Scholastically, Group D people tend to have likes and dislikes which often are peculiar and seemingly contradictory. Group D people have a preference for topics in the Humanities and Social Sciences. They tend to have almost a dislike for the Sciences. On the other hand, they prefer reading assignments and laboratory projects over lectures and writing assignments. Consistent with their low aggression scores, Group D people tend to prefer lectures more than self-directed work and discussions more than lectures. Very few Group D people will pursue theoretical issues; the majority seems to prefer practical application. Teacher guidance and direction will be most effective in the areas of establishing guidelines, feedback, deadlines, and generally structuring the Group D student's progress. They will not have severe difficulty selecting areas of interest, but motivation to achieve might appear to be lacking. Exams tend to be occasions of mild to moderate anxiety. Their preference is for multiple-choice question tests, perhaps, because they tend to perform most adequately with a multiple-choice question.

What should be done with questions 37, 38, 39 and 40?

Since the SPAS was designed to be used as a learning experience, the last four items in the questionnaire were left blank in order for the examiner to have the opportunity of preparing questions just like the psychologist must. These four questions are not scored as part of the test, but the subject should respond to them. The examiner can compare the answers on these items to the trend of answers in the first 36 items.

The four items which the examiner should prepare are of a true-false nature. The subject should respond by marking "false" if he does not agree that the statement applies to him and "true" if the statement does apply to him. The examiner should remember that the statements should be either aggressive or nonaggressive so that they could be used to distinguish one group from another. Be careful to avoid a "response set," that is, don't make the aggressive person always respond by marking "true" and the nonaggressive by marking "false." An idea of how these statements should be worded can be gained by looking at items 31 to 36.

SPAS Hand Scoring Stencil

Punch out the X's. Place this stencil over the subject's answer sheet and count the marks made by the subject which show through the punched out holes.

1.	X	B	?		21.	X	B	?
2.	X	B	?		22.	A	X	?
3.	A	X	?		23.	X	B	?
4.	X	B	?		24.	X	B	?
5.	A	X	?		25.	A	X	?
6.	X	B	?		26.	A	X	?
7.	A	X	?		27.	X	B	?
8.	X	B	?		28.	X	B	?
9.	A	X	?		29.	A	X	?
10.	A	X	?		30.	X	B	?
11.	X	B	?		31.	X	B	?
12.	X	B	?		32.	X	B	?
13.	A	X	?		33.	A	X	?
14.	X	B	?		34.	A	X	?
15.	A	X	?		35.	X	B	?
16.	X	B	?		36.	A	B	?
17.	A	X	?		37.	A	B	?
18.	A	X	?		38.	A	B	?
19.	X	B	?		39.	A	B	?
20.	A	X	?		40.	A	B	?

SPAS Answer Sheet

Indicate your choice by marking an X. For example: A 🅧 ?

1.	A	B	?		21.	A	B	?
2.	A	B	?		22.	A	B	?
3.	A	B	?		23.	A	B	?
4.	A	B	?		24.	A	B	?
5.	A	B	?		25.	A	B	?
6.	A	B	?		26.	A	B	?
7.	A	B	?		27.	A	B	?
8.	A	B	?		28.	A	B	?
9.	A	B	?		29.	A	B	?
10.	A	B	?		30.	A	B	?
11.	A	B	?		31.	A	B	?
12.	A	B	?		32.	A	B	?
13.	A	B	?		33.	A	B	?
14.	A	B	?		34.	A	B	?
15.	A	B	?		35.	A	B	?
16.	A	B	?		36.	A	B	?
17.	A	B	?		37.	A	B	?
18.	A	B	?		38.	A	B	?
19.	A	B	?		39.	A	B	?
20.	A	B	?		40.	A	B	?

Simulated Personality Assessment Scale (SPAS)

Question Booklet

(Student Form)

Please answer each of the questions below. Simply respond by marking on the answer sheet the choice which is *most true for you.* Do not be concerned with right or wrong answers—only what is true for you. There are three choices, "A" "B" or "?." Mark only one choice. The third choice is always "?," which you should use if you cannot decide between the other two choices. Work at a normal rate; there is no time limit. Every item must be answered.

1. Which do you prefer to watch on television?
   A. Football
   B. Drama
   C. ?

2. What do you do when you are angry at someone?
   A. Say something to the object of your anger
   B. Suppress your anger
   C. ?

3. What do you usually do when you first arrive at a party?
   A. Wait for the host and hostess to come to you
   B. Introduce yourself to the host and hostess
   C. ?

4. After meeting the host and hostess at a party, what do you do?
   A. Seek out someone you know to talk to
   B. Introduce yourself to a stranger
   C. ?

5. What do most people do when they see people fighting?
   A. Move away from the scene of the fight
   B. Move closer to see the fight
   C. ?

6. What do you do when you see two dogs fighting?
   A. Move closer and watch the fight
   B. Ignore the fight and not watch
   C. ?

7. If a roommate used your last clean towel, and you did not have a clean towel for your bath, what would you do?
   A. Forget the incident
   B. Mention the incident to the roommate
   C. ?

8. In your opinion, should police officers force people to obey laws?
   A. Yes, force is necessary
   B. No, people should learn to obey without force
   C. ?

9. If a professor made a mistake while calculating your grade would you:
   A. Go to your advisor for help in the matter
   B. Demand an appointment in order to discuss the matter
   C. ?

10. If you discovered a pen on someone else's desk, and that pen was like one you had which disappeared, would you:
    A. Ask for the pen
    B. Take the pen
    C. ?

11. If an assignment is given out on Monday morning and is due on Friday morning, would you:
    A. Begin working as soon as possible
    B. Delay as long as possible
    C. ?

12. If you could change the present educational system would you:
    A. Like to be allowed to speak out more about your education
    B. Be able to go your own quiet way
    C. ?

13. What do you do in a restaurant when the waiter does not come to your table?
    A. Leave the restaurant
    B. Seek out a waiter
    C. ?

14. When you drive up to a gas station pump for gas and the attendant does not come out to your car right away, do you:
    A. Blow your horn
    B. Leave the station
    C. ?

15. If a waiter told you the tip wasn't good enough for the service, would you:
    A. Ignore him
    B. Tell him the service wasn't so good either
    C. ?

16. What do you do at a party when you see a member of the opposite sex whom you would like to meet?
    A. Approach the person and introduce yourself
    B. Wait for the proper moment for an introduction to occur
    C. ?

17. If a dog bit into the back of your leg and held on, would you:
    A. Pinch the dog's nose and upper jaw to make him release his hold
    B. Hit the dog to make him release his hold
    C. ?

18. Which would you rather do?
    A. Play cards (bridge, poker or whatever)
    B. Play baseball (boy's or girl's variety)
    C. ?

19. Would you say that you:
    A. Eat rapidly
    B. Eat slowly
    C. ?

20. Which would you rather be?
    A. A doctor or nurse
    B. A panelist star on a television show
    C. ?

21. In an emergency do you:
    A. Act quickly while thinking out the problem
    B. Act slowly in order to think out the problem before acting
    C. ?

22. Would you rather:
    A. Listen to someone of equal intelligence to you
    B. Talk to someone of equal intelligence to you
    C. ?

23. Do you prefer church services where:
    A. Prayers are said aloud by the entire congregation
    B. Prayers are said silently by each member of the congregation
    C. ?

24. If you saw someone breaking into a store, would you:
    A. Telephone the police
    B. Ignore the situation
    C. ?

25. Which do you prefer to work with:
    A. Paint and a brush
    B. Hammer, nails and a saw
    C. ?

26. Do you prefer to:
    A. Be told the answer to a perplexing problem
    B. Be allowed to seek out the answer yourself
    C. ?

27. If a public speaker makes a statement with which you disagree, do you:
    A. Speak out during the question and answer period
    B. Talk to a friend about the statement afterwards
    C. ?

28. If you had to be a construction worker, would you rather be a:
    A. Bulldozer operator
    B. Surveying assistant
    C. ?

29. Which job would you choose to do first?
    A. Wash windows
    B. Trim shrubbery
    C. ?

30. Do you often spend Saturdays doing odd jobs?
    A. Yes
    B. No
    C. ?

The next set of questions have true-false choices.

31. I am likely to say what I think, rather than be "nice."
    A. True
    B. False
    C. ?

32. I cannot tolerate situations where I must be a passive observer.
    A. True
    B. False
    C. ?

33. I would rather watch children play than join in their activity.
    A. True
    B. False
    C. ?

34. Going to a concert is more fun than going to a picnic.
    A. True
    B. False
    C. ?

35. Most people (like me) want more participation in local government.
    A. True
    B. False
    C. ?

36. My choice of clothes is based more on fashion than function.
    A. True
    B. False
    C. ?

37. _____ :
    A. True
    B. False
    C. ?

38. _____ :
    A. True
    B. False
    C. ?

39. _____ :
    A. True
    B. False
    C. ?

40. _____ :
    A. True
    B. False
    C. ?

SPAS Interview Guidelines Sheet

After the subject's scores have been explained and the interpretation of the results read, the examiner should ask the subject to respond to the following questions. The questions should be asked in an oral interview. The major question is given first with the follow-up or secondary questions in ( ).

1. Do you think the test was really a good measure of aggression and indecision in your case? (Why?) (Why not?) (Can you remember parts of the test which were good examples of measures of aggression? indecision?)

2. Do you agree with the description of your nonacademic behavior? [The examiner may have to read the interpretation again.] (Why?) (Why not?) (Can you give specific examples of your behavior which support or deny the interpretation?)

3. Do you agree with the description of your academic behavior? (Why?) (Why not?) (What particular parts are incorrect? correct?) (Can you give examples of your behavior which support or deny the academic interpretation?)

Teaching Strategy Checklist

After you have interpreted the results of the SPAS, you should use the information as if you were a teacher. In this case you are to write a proposed teaching strategy which would be used with the person to whom you administered the test. Imagine that the person who took the SPAS is a student in your class. Now write a proposed teaching strategy based on the information gained from the test. Here is a checklist which you can use to help structure your teaching strategy.

When writing your teaching strategy, did you consider:

1. A description of the subject and scores

2. Did you consider the information in the test manual under the section, "Describe the characteristics of the persons in the four groups." Specifically, did you consider the subject's characteristics in regard to:

    1. degree of participation
    2. readiness to enter into activities
    3. selection of activities
    4. reaction to aversive situations
    5. topics or subject matter to be studied
    6. teaching methods
    7. theoretical versus practical emphasis
    8. commitment to selected activities
    9. examination type and level of performance
    10. anxiety reaction to examinations

3. In addition you should mention anything pertinent said by the subject during the interview.

Teaching Strategy Sample

Following is an example of a teaching strategy based on the results of the SPAS. Use the checklist above to determine if all the pertinent information was used.*

The SPAS was administered to a female college sophomore. Her raw scores were: Aggression = 20, Indecision = 13. This placed her in quadrant B, or with the B Group. Group B people are considered as being high aggression and high indecision.

* A hint: one item on the checklist was not mentioned. Once you identify that item, decide what a teacher could do in regard to that characteristic.

It can be expected that she will have some difficulty selecting activities when given freedom. With this in mind, she will be given a list of optional exercises from which to choose, and counseling during the selection period will be readily available. Should she avoid making a selection, a deadline will be imposed.

The options given to her should permit the investigation of theoretical issues and practical application. It is anticipated that she will prefer to work on subjects related to either Science or Social Sciences, so initially the options should be from those two areas. If so desired, in the later exercises the Humanities could be worked into Social Science or Science subjects. Learning should include small group discussions and independent work. A minimum amount of lecture will be used with her. It would be useful to place her in a group of 3 to 4 students who are more decisive and who might impose structure and scheduling to which she would conform. If the assignment includes multiple reading activities, they should be sequenced for her ahead of time, and a reading schedule set up for her use.

It is expected that she will prefer essay-type examinations, and since she performs best on those type, it is also expected that she will receive the greatest reinforcement if an essay exam is given. Essay exams might also keep anxiety down to a minimum, therefore, perhaps, giving a more accurate measure of her learning than other exam types. Evaluation of her learning is likely to be rather difficult in view of the tendency of Group B people to expend energy on a variety of activities, therefore, probably learning a little about a lot of things, rather than a lot about one thing.

♦ SUMMARY

If you look back over Unit One, you will see that we began by considering the vague, amorphous concept called "personality." We moved to a consideration of the meaning of personality and, more important, to the structure of that concept. Since many psychologists prefer to work with more concrete parts rather than the abstract whole, the concept of personality was broken down into parts called behavior traits. Traits, supposedly, can be measured, and the degree to which an individual possesses a trait can be related to various abilities that individual might or might not have.

In the experience aspect of this Unit, you were given the opportunity to use the SPAS to deal with personality as certain psychologists might. The recommended procedure was to prepare yourself for administering the SPAS by reading the test manual and taking the SPAS yourself. Once prepared, you were to give the SPAS to someone else and interpret the results. From the results, you were to derive a teaching strategy.

Now, if you have completed the suggested procedures and accomplished the Experience Objectives, it is time to consider what *you* now know about personality and learning. Did your experience lead you to believe that behavior traits are *real* phenomena, or, perhaps, is personality something else entirely?

If your subject didn't particularly agree with the results of the SPAS, you should consider the possibility that the test was not valid. What does it mean to say that a test is not valid? In simplest terms it means that the test does not measure what it is supposed to measure. How can you tell whether a test is valid or not? This question leads us to an important aspect of standardized test preparation. The author of the test should explain in the test manual how he knows the test is valid. The SPAS is based on *construct validity*. This means that a construct like aggression was identified, and it seems to the author of the test that the questions in the test measure that construct, but he cannot produce data which support that opinion. Are you willing to accept that type of validity? Does it seem to you that aggression is really being measured?

There is another aspect of standardized test making which should be mentioned in the test manual: *the reliability of the test*. If your subject said that he would answer the questions differently at different times, then he was saying that the test was probably not reliable. There are a variety of ways of measuring reliability, and the author of the test should tell you in the manual how he evaluated the reliability of the test and just how reliable it is. A rubber yardstick is not very reliable because a piece of wood which is twelve inches long by a metal yardstick might be thirteen inches one time, fourteen inches another, and so on with a rubber measuring instrument. How reliable is the SPAS? Does the author of the test mention reliability in the test manual? You should have grave doubts about a test which does not have validity and reliability data to support it. Would you use an instrument like the SPAS in a classroom for helping you work with your students?

There are a wealth of questions which loom up when one considers using a personality assessment instrument in the classroom. For instance, is it practical in a class of 20 to 30 students? If most student's scores fall in a range where distinct identification is not possible, the scores are of little use. Or are they? Can you or would you want to use trends in scores to make instructional decisions? Why not?

Research psychologists have not provided clear-cut answers to the questions posed in this summary. The answers in most instances depend upon a myriad of variables peculiar to different situations. You probably answered some of the questions with, "Sometimes, yes, and sometimes, no. It depends." But, upon what does it depend? Well, for better or for worse, one variable upon which it depends is you, the teacher. You may reject this psychological approach to learning and teaching, or you may wish to embrace it as one of your techniques. Your personal reasons are supported by experiential data, and, hopefully, your rationale for rejection or selection is now reasonably sound and scholarly.

If your interest in the personality approach to learning and teaching was stimulated, or if you simply want more information on which to make decisions, the following Suggested Further Activities and References might be helpful.

♦ SUGGESTED ADDITIONAL ACTIVITIES

If you are particularly interested in approaching problems of education from a personality assessment standpoint, you might want to engage in one of the following experiences:

1. Consider the question, Can I subjectively place a person in one of the "Groups" without (or before) giving the test? Many teachers believe that they can evaluate a student's personality as well without a test as they could with the test. What do you think about your own ability to evaluate the traits, aggression and indecision, in another person? You might want to select four or five people you know fairly well and guess their group before administering the test. You might find that you can guess at their scores as accurately as the test. A second question related to the previous one is, How well can people identify their own groups? In order to answer the latter question, you might want to explain the various characteristics of the groups and ask the subjects to rate themselves before they take the test. Interesting discussions often arise around the question, How well do I know myself?

2. Consider the possibility that subjects falsify their answers for one reason or another and, therefore, invalidate the test. One method of evaluating such an hypothesis would be to ask several subjects to take the test and "lie to make yourself look good like the model person." Within a short time afterward, ask them to take the test a second time and answer the questions honestly, or as if they were taking the test to really evaluate themselves. Should the scores from the two tests be very similar, we can't say with any certainty that the subjects have a tendency to falsify answers, but an interesting discussion should certainly ensure regarding why the results were so similar.

3. Prepare a straight-forward questionnaire with questions like:

    Which do you prefer? Lectures_____ Recitations_____ Other_____

    Do you experience exam panic? Yes_____ No_____

    Give the questionnaire to subjects before administering the SPAS. Evaluate from your small sample of subjects whether or not the predictions about "Groups" behavior in the test manual agree with the results of your questionnaire.

◆ SUGGESTED ADDITIONAL READINGS

For Basic Information About Personality

Geiwitz, P. James. *Non-Freudian Personality Theories.* Belmont, Calif.: Brooks/
Cole Publishing Company, 1969.
Kelly, E. Lowell. *Assessment of Human Characteristics.* Belmont, Calif.: Brooks/
Cole Publishing Company, 1967.
Lazarus, Richard S. *Personality and Adjustment.* Englewood Cliffs, New Jersey:
Prentice-Hall, Inc., 1963.

For Detailed Information About Specific Theories of Personality

Allport, Gordon W. *Pattern and Growth in Personality.* New York: Holt, Rinehart
and Winston, 1961.
Guilford, J. P. *Personality.* New York: McGraw-Hill, 1959.
Loehlin, J. C. *Computer Models of Personality.* New York: Random House, 1968.
Mischel, W. *Personality and Assessment.* New York: Wiley, 1968.
Rogers, C. R. *On Becoming a Person.* Boston: Houghton Mifflin, 1961.

For Specific Studies Relating Personality Variables to Education

Amidon, E., and Flanders, N. A. "The Effects of Direct and Indirect Teacher In-
fluence on Dependent-prone Students Learning Geometry." *Journal of
Abnormal Social Psychology* 52(1961):286–291.
Grimes, J. W., and Allinsmith, W. "Compulsivity, Anxiety and School Achieve-
ment." *Merrill-Palmer Quarterly* 7(1961):247–272. (Available from John-
son Reprint Corporation, New York, N.Y.)
Kagan, J. "Reflection-impulsivity and Reading Ability in Primary Grade Children."
Child Development 36(1965):609–628.
Kagan, J., Pearson, L., and Welch, L. "Conceptual Impulsivity and Inductive
Reasoning." *Child Development* 37(1966):583–594.
Kagan, J., and Mussen, P. H. "Dependency Themes on the TAT and Group Con-
formity." *Journal of Consulting Psychology* 20(1956):19–27.
Livson, N. and Nichols, T. F. "The Relation of Control to Overt Aggression and
Dependency." *Journal of Abnormal Social Psychology* 55(1957):66–71.
Neel, Ann F. "The Relationship of Authoritarian Personality to Learning: F-Scale
Scores Compared to Classroom Performance." *Journal of Educational Psy-
chology* 50(1959):195–199.
Neville, D., Pfost, P., and Dobbs, V. "The Relationship Between Test Anxiety and
Silent Reading Gain." *American Educational Research Journal* 4(1967):
45–50.
Walberg, H. J., and Ahlgren, A. "Predictors of Social Environment of Learning."
American Educational Research Journal 7(1970):153–168.

UNIT 2

Intelligence

♦ BACKGROUND

The general purpose of this unit is to acquaint you with that part of the human being which we call intelligence. Many educational psychologists have spent their entire careers studying the human intellect. Intelligence has often been viewed as the most important difference between human beings in a formal school environment. Most people will agree that the human is the most intelligent animal on earth, but what exactly do we mean? How do we define "intelligence?" How do we measure it? Among other activities in this unit, you will have the opportunity to explore the theory of intelligence set forth by a noted psychologist, to administer an intelligence test similar to the standardized batteries used in public schools, and to develop a test item of your own which you feel measures some aspect of human intelligence. But, initially, let us look at some questions about intelligence.

Why should teachers or prospective teachers be concerned with a psychologist's view of intelligence?

The notion of intelligence as it is used by the layman is much like the idea of personality. It is a vague construct which often becomes responsible for a variety of good and bad behaviors. For example, it is often the case that a child who does well in school is later expected to continue to do well "because he is more intelligent than the other students." Or the student from a low-income family who performs poorly in school is often passed off as "not very intelligent . . . just like the rest of the family." An observer in the typical teacher's lounge in most schools will in a short time have a long list of the varied uses of the term, intelligence. But, what do they mean by intelligence? Is the term used carefully and selectively? It would seem prudent for the teacher who uses the term frequently to have more than just a passing knowledge of its meaning. The information psychologists have learned about intelligence could help the teacher deal with this concept more accurately and succinctly than was possible in the past.

What does the psychologist mean when he refers to "intelligence"?

To help answer that question let us extend the analogy between personality and intelligence. In Unit One we said that psychologists do not all agree on one definition of personality. That same statement is true for intelligence. Some psychologists deal with intelligence as an index of the individual's ability to take in information. Other psychologists adhere to the idea that intelligence is simply one's ability to adapt or accommodate to new information. Still others deal with intelligence in a manner similar to personality; that is, they break it down into *factors* or *abilities*. In this latter view, the structure of intelligence is more important than the definition, just as was the case with personality. Factors or abilities are often derived as a result of statistical manipulation of the results of standardized tests. It is beyond the scope and purpose of this book to explain the methods used to identify factors in this way, but the reader concerned with the techniques used should refer to the Suggested Readings at the end of this Unit. However, it is important for the reader to understand that a large number of psychologists are not content to just deal with the abstract construct, "intelligence," but, rather, prefer to work with more concrete factors which can be identified through the use of testing procedures.

What are "factors" of intelligence?

For the sake of simplicity, we will describe factors of intelligence as those parts or components which go together to make up the entity we call intelligence.

What factors have been identified by psychologists?

Unfortunately, it is not possible to say that a certain number of intelligence factors have been identified by researchers. At least this is not true in the same sense that chemical elements have been identified and placed on the atomic weights charts. For instance, an individual researcher might follow strategies and theoretical postulates which lead him to propose a certain set of factors with a certain set of names for the factors, but there is no guarantee that another psychologist in another situation will agree that the factors are a part of intelligence nor is he likely to accept the names given to the factors. To help the reader achieve a better understanding of how a psychologist works with intelligence through a factor approach, we will investigate the particular model of intelligence set forth by J. P. Guilford.[1]

What are the factors of intelligence according to Guilford?

Guilford has identified 120 different factors of intelligence which can be broken down in the following manner: Suppose a set of tests which were supposed to measure factors of intelligence differed in regard to the material or *content* within each test item. It would be reasonable for the test designer to try to divide up various factors of intelligence along the dimension, content. That is part of what Guilford did. The different aspects of content which he identified were called *figural, symbolic, semantic,* and *behavioral.* Therefore, a test item might have material in it which is figural in nature like an item consisting of only geometric forms. A geometric form item would have a vastly different basic content from an item which tested the subject's ability to use words and their meanings. This latter item would have content of a semantic nature.

To complicate matters, however, other dimensions besides content also suggest logical factoring. One such dimension is called *operation.* In the operation dimension, factors are divided according to the task or operation which the subject performs. For example, if the test item demands that the subject remember something that he saw briefly, then the task is one of remembering. Remembering has been called *memory* by Guilford. On the other hand, if you present a picture of a cow and a pig to a child and he can tell you that they are different, then you would say that the child can recognize the difference between the two animals. Such a task would involve *cognition.* Memory and cognition are two of the five divisions under the dimension, operation. The other three divisions are *divergent production, convergent production,* and *evaluation.*

Yet another dimension can be used for factoring. This one has been labeled *product.* Along the product dimension we find such factors as *units, classes, relations, systems, transformations,* and *implications.* It seems fairly obvious that a test item in which the subject identifies the difference between two geometric forms is working with units, while a test item which calls for the placing of several figures into groups with common characteristics is working with classes. On such a basis, the factoring of intelligence along the dimension, product, also seems logical.

1. J. P. Guilford, *The Nature of Human Intelligence* (New York: McGraw-Hill, 1967).

So Guilford initially divided intelligence into the three major dimensions, content, operations, and products, and subdivided these major categories into 15 subcategories.

How does Guilford combine the three dimensions for factoring intelligence?

Guilford devised a rather ingenious visual representation of intelligence factors by utilizing a three dimensional cube. You can see in Figure 2.1 how he used each of the three faces of the cube to represent one of the dimensions.

How are factors identified within Guilford's model?

A quick calculation will tell you that there are 120 cells in the 5 x 6 x 4 cube. Each one of these 120 cells is named according to a combination of Operation—Content—Product. Each cell represents a factor of the concept, intelligence. For example, one factor would be "memory of symbolic units." The Operation would be "memory," the Content would be "symbolic" and the Product would be "units." An example of a possible test item for measuring memory of symbolic units would be one in which the subject was asked to recall a list of nonsense words after a brief exposure to the list. Other types of test items are available for other factors within the cube.

If a test is based on a "factor" notion of intelligence, how is an "IQ" score derived?

If a test battery had items which measured 80 of the 120 factors in Guilford's notion of intelligence, these 80 items would measure intelligence only according to a particular factor approach. That is to say—a subject's total score on the 80 items would be the closest possible measurement we could make of intelligence according to Guilford's definition. However, not all items use common units of measurement; some test items measure time while others might measure frequency or accuracy. It is just not practical or convenient to report 80 different scores for one subject; so a method for converting the scores is necessary. This is where one part of the IQ or intelligence quotient comes into the picture. Different scores from different test items are converted to a common unit called *mental age* which is given in months. Again, it is beyond the scope and purpose of this book to explain how the mental age scores are derived and converted, but several of the books in the Suggested Readings section of this unit explain the procedure quite adequately.

In addition to mental age score, each living person has a *chronological age* score which is simply the number of months which have elapsed since

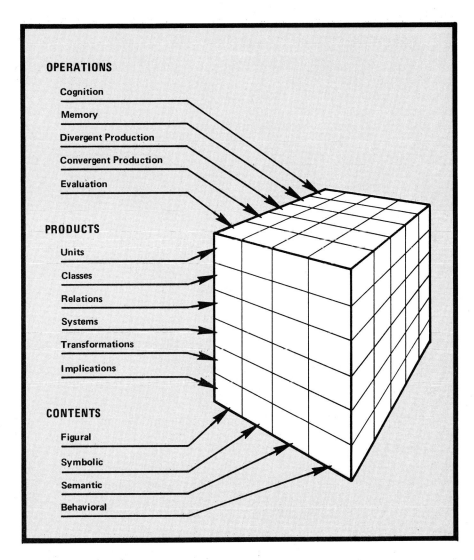

Figure 2.1 Model of the structure of intellect. Reprinted from: Guilford, J. P. "Intelligence: 1965 Model," *The American Psychologist,* January, 1966, 20, p. 21, by permission of the author. Copyright 1966 by the American Psychological Association, and reproduced by permission.

the person was born. IQ, then, is a ratio between mental age (MA) and chronological age (CA) scores and that ratio score is multiplied by 100. For example, if a student takes the 80 item test and achieves a mental age score of 85, and is seven years and one month or 85 months old, then his IQ is calculated by dividing 85 by 85 and multiplying the answer by 100.

$$\frac{85}{85} \times 100 = 100$$

His IQ is 100, or average for his age.

The important concept to remember here is that the final indication of the individual's intelligence is based on a theoretical notion of what intelligence is and also on a set of standardized test items which supposedly measure the parts of intelligence. In short, it all depends on a test.

♦ AN EXPERIENCE

How does all of this background information relate to the experience in this unit?

The experience in this unit involves the administration of a ten item test which supposedly could measure some factors of intelligence. Whether the test items actually do measure intelligence or not is something you will have to decide. In addition, you will create a test item of your own which should measure another factor of intelligence. The major purpose in such an experience is for you to recognize what a psychologist actually does when he attempts to measure a vague concept like intelligence. The major emphasis in this experience is upon the definition of intelligence—as exemplified by the test items—but we are not concerned with measuring IQ. In this regard, your test subject will probably ask, How did I do? Remember, you are concerned with the larger concept of intelligence, not with individual performances. In response to his question, simply say that you have no way of comparing him to others, and that he probably performed as well as he could, which was all that was required. The Experience Objectives which follow will give you a better picture of your task.

Experience Objectives

1. You should prepare one test item to be included with the Simulated Intelligence Test Battery.

2. You should write a description of the additional test item from Experience Objective 1, a script for instructions to be given with this test item, a description of what aspect of intelligence is being tested, a paragraph hypothesizing the relationship between this one test item and others in existence. This is all done with the help of the *Additional Test Item Guidelines Form.*

3. You should administer the Simulated Intelligence Test Battery. (The subject can be another college student).

4. You should write a description of the test administration experience which will include:
    a. description of subject
    b. description of test environment
    c. subjective analysis of subject's reaction to being tested
    d. performance scores on test items

Suggested Procedure for Achieving the Experience Objectives

1. Read over the Simulated Intelligence Test Battery Script and attempt the test items yourself. Remember, do not write on the test—you only have one.
2. Prepare an additional test item of your own design to be used with the Simulated Intelligence Test Battery.
3. Use the Additional Test Item Guidelines form to help you write a description of the test item you developed.
4. Administer the Simulated Intelligence Test Battery.
5. Use the Test Administration Report Guidelines form to help you write a description of the testing experience.

Progress Chart

Activity	Check each space when completed.
1. Preview test battery	_____
2. Additional test item preparation	_____
3. Additional test item guidelines form	_____
4. Administer Simulated Test Battery	_____
5. Test Administration Report Guideline	_____

Additional Test Item Guidelines Form

1. Give a general description of your own test item. Draw pictures, graphs, diagrams, etc. as used with the test item.

2. Write out the exact words an examiner would use when giving instructions for this test item.

3. What specific aspect of intelligence do you think you are testing, i.e., visual memory? creativity? divergent thinking? combinations of several? Explain why you think this is true.

4. How do you think this item relates to others you have seen? Might there be a positive correlation with the maze? tracking? A negative correlation with auditory memory?

Test Administration Report Guidelines

After you have administered the Simulated Intelligence Test Battery, you should prepare a written report of the experience. The questions below will aid you.

1. Describe the test subject, i.e., sex, age, etc.

2. Describe the environment in which the test was administered. Ex. Room, furniture used, light, noise, disturbances.

3. Describe the behaviors (non-test) of the subject before, during, *and after* the test experience.

4. Attach the score sheet to your report with any pertinent comments you wish to make.

5. Do you think you obtained an accurate measure of this individual's "intelligence?" (Use your own definition of intelligence.)

SCRIPT FOR SIMULATED INTELLIGENCE TEST BATTERY

The Maze

The first test I am going to give you is called the Maze. You are to place your pencil on the X in the center of the maze and trace a line to the other X outside the Maze. You may not cross any lines or touch any lines. You may not pick up your pencil. I will record the amount of time it takes you to finish. Are there any questions? If not . . . begin.

The Tracking Test

In this test you are to circle all the figures which look like this (point to the & on the sheet). There are ten in all. I will record the amount of time it takes you to finish this test. You will be penalized for errors. Are there any questions? If not, begin.

The Auditory Memory Test

I am going to say some numbers in a certain order. You are to say them back to me in the same order. For example, if I say 1, 3, 4; you would say . . .

    9 5 3
    6 8 4 1
    9 1 7 6 9
    6 9 1 4 7 3
    2 6 2 4 1 9 6
    7 9 5 2 1 7 0 6
    5 3 8 1 7 4 2 6 7
    8 6 5 1 0 3 5 2 7 8
    2 4 3 8 9 7 1 0 5 9 3
    3 4 2 9 1 8 6 9 5 7 8 5

Auditory Memory Reverse

This time I am going to say some numbers and you are to say them back to me in reverse order. For example, if I say 1, 4, 5; you say 5, 4, 1.

8 5 3

6 8 4 0

1 9 7 8 5

5 7 3 4 1 0

8 6 0 1 5 3 8

3 6 7 9 1 5 4 3

9 4 7 1 6 4 0 2 6

Visual Memory Test

Here are three blocks. I am going to point to the blocks in a certain order. You are to point to them in the same order after I finish.

3 2 3

1 3 2

2 1 2 3

2 1 3 2 1

3 1 2 3 1 2

1 3 1 2 1 2 3

3 2 3 2 1 3 2 1

1 3 2 3 1 2 1 3 2

3 2 3 1 3 2 3 1 3 1

The Fluency Test

In this next test I am going to give you the signal to begin, and you are to begin naming words as fast as you can. You will have one minute to name as many words as possible. You may not use number sequences. You may not use sentences or phrases. A word may not be used more than once.

The Literacy Test

In this test you will be given one minute to write as much as you can about a given topic. Which topic would you like to write about: animals, plants, oceans, or countries? You must write complete sentences. Your goal is to write as many words as possible, but as few sentences as possible. In other words, you are to write as long sentences as you can. Conjunctive sentences are counted as two or more sentences. For example, if you connect two short sentences with an ''and,'' it will be counted as two sentences. Your score will be the total number of words written divided by the total number of sentences written.

Color Naming Test

For this next test I want you to name as many colors as possible in 30 seconds. A color may be named only once, but variations are possible, like red, cardinal, scarlet, etc.

Word Formation Test

There are ten letters on this sheet of paper. You are to write as many words as possible in one minute. The words can be of any length.

Alphabetizing

There are some words written on this sheet of paper. You are to write these words in alphabetical order from top to bottom. I will record the amount of time it takes you to write them. You will be penalized for each mistake.

Simulated Intelligence Test Battery Score Sheet

1. The Maze: score_____. (Score is total time in seconds to escape from maze. Five (5) seconds are added for each error, i.e. line touched or crossed, pencil lifted.)

2. The Tracking Test: score_____. (Score is total time in seconds to complete track. Five (5) seconds are added for each symbol missed or incorrectly included.)

3. The Auditory Memory Test: score_____. (Score is the total number of digits in the *last correctly repeated* sequence. Examiner stops when two (2) sequences in a row are repeated incorrectly.)

4. The Auditory Memory Reverse Test: score_____. (Score is calculated in the same manner as Auditory Memory Test 3 above.)

5. Visual Memory Test: score_____. (Score is calculated in the same manner as 3 & 4 above.)

6. The Fluency Test: score_____. (Score total number of words recited.)

7. The Literacy Test: score_____. (Score total number of words written divided by total number sentences written.)

8. Color Naming Test: score_____. (Score number of words named.)

9. The Word Formation Test: score_____. (Score number of words written.)

10. Alphabetizing Test: score_____. (Score time in seconds: five (5) seconds for each mistake.)

Your own test item: score_____.

Simulated Intelligence Test Battery

On the next few pages you will find materials necessary for the following tests:

1. Maze (In addition, you will need a stopwatch or at least, a watch with a sweep-second hand.)
2. Tracking (A clock is needed here also.)
3. Visual Memory
4. The Literacy Test
5. Word Formation Test
6. Alphabetizing Test

Note: The other tests in the battery do not require special materials other than paper and pencil.

Maze

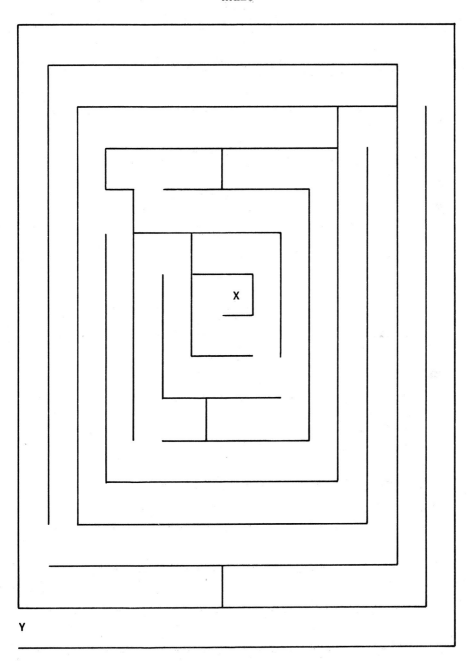

Tracking

&

JLDCKLFJLRSCUTIYR&BNHGFRDESWATGYHUJIK
PLOKMIJNUHBYGVTFCRDXESZWA&XTFCYGVBHGFD
LKJHGFDSAZXCVBNMPOIUYTREEWRTYUIOPLKJ&JH
QAZWSX&EDCRFVTGBYHN&UJMIKOLPOLIKUJYHTGT
PL,IJNUHBYGVTFCRDXESZAWTGYHBNJIKMOLKMUJ&
OKMIJNUHBGVTFCRDXRDXTFCYGVYBBUJNMKJUJKMN
PLQKMIJNUHBYGVTFCRDXESZAWERTYUIOPLKJHGFDSA
O&LKIJMNHGFDSAZXCVBNM,LKJH&JHGTGTGYHUJIK
POIUYTREWQASDFGHJKLPOIUYTREWASDFGH&HJKI
FOIUYT&YUJHYUJIKJHGFDS WERTYUIOPLKJHGFDUIO

Visual Memory

The Literacy Test

Word Formation Test

I B E O T F L M Z P

—————————————————   —————————————————

—————————————————   —————————————————

—————————————————   —————————————————

—————————————————   —————————————————

—————————————————   —————————————————

—————————————————   —————————————————

—————————————————   —————————————————

—————————————————   —————————————————

—————————————————   —————————————————

—————————————————   —————————————————

—————————————————   —————————————————

—————————————————   —————————————————

—————————————————   —————————————————

—————————————————   —————————————————

—————————————————   —————————————————

Alphabetizing

BOAT   _____

WHEEL   _____

HORSE   _____

ANCHOR   _____

SHEEP   _____

ME   _____

FIDDLE   _____

NOON   _____

CAR   _____

TINGLE   _____

HOUSE   _____

YIELD   _____

GARAGE   _____

ABOUT   _____

FIT   _____

KITCHEN   _____

KART   _____

♦ SUMMARY

The purpose of this unit was to expose the reader to the intelligence approach to learning and teaching. Intelligence can have many meanings; so a psychologist who emphasizes intelligence when he looks at problems of learning and teaching might be using one of many different meanings. The particular concept of intelligence which was stressed in this unit was a factor model. The key to a factor model of intelligence is that the human intellect is supposedly made up of several components or parts which become the factors of intelligence. Guilford's model for the structure of intelligence was used as an illustration of one psychologist's conceptualization. Since individual factors are usually associated with a particular type of task, tests which are standardized instances of those tasks become a common means for attaining a measure of intelligence.

A psychologist who considers intelligence from a factor standpoint, and who also considers test items to be a legitimate measure of those factors will find himself preparing test items and administering tests. That is the basis for the experience in this unit. The reader was given the opportunity to administer a battery of test items to a subject. The actual score attained by the subject was irrelevant to the task at hand. On the other hand, there are a number of highly relevant questions which the reader should be considering at this point.

The most important question which each and every teacher must answer individually is, Do tests like this measure intelligence as *I* see it? Another way of saying it might be, Am I willing to accept a notion of intelligence like the one exemplified by the Simulated Test Battery? If the answer to both of these questions is "no," then Why not? Intelligence could be something more than just the subject's ability to perform well on a test. But, if it is, what difference does that make to the classroom teacher? Is the version of intelligence exemplified by the Simulated Test Battery adequate for use in the day-to-day business of educating students? Again, if not, what are you going to do with IQs and other information about a student's intelligence which are based on scores from tests similar to the Simulated Test Battery? You could use the individual test item scores to help a student develop a particular factor. You could use individual test item scores to identify strengths a student might possess. But there are further questions you should consider about your experience.

In regard to the actual experience of administering a test battery: Did *you* become nervous when it was time to begin? Did the subject exhibit fear of a testing situation? What did you do to alleviate your or his fear? Why? What evidence can you draw upon to show that you reacted correctly? Would other test administrators react in the same manner? All of these questions imply that you as the person manipulating the measurement instrument might have had an influence upon the subject's performance. Imagine the most introverted individual you know. Now, imagine that person giving the test battery to your subject. Would the scores be comparable to those you attained? If so, then the Simulated Test Battery is a reliable measurement instrument. If not, then the battery is, perhaps, like a rubber yardstick, but, on the other hand, a rubber yardstick is perhaps better than none at all. And, perhaps, it is possible to teach a variety of people to measure reliably and accurately with a rubber yardstick.

The position you can now assume regarding intelligence should reflect your thought about the experience in this unit and the answers to some of the questions posed in this Summary. There is a wealth of literature available which illustrates the various psychological approaches to the single concept, intelligence. Some of the more popular material written is listed in the Suggested Readings Section of this unit. If, as a result of seeing how a psychologist approaches intelligence you are somewhat confused about what intelligence "really" is, then, maybe, it is a healthy state to be in. Seeking additional information is often a method for bringing order out of confusion.

♦ SUGGESTED ADDITIONAL ACTIVITIES

Some extended experience with intelligence testing might provide the type of information you need to decide what role intelligence will play in your approach to learning and teaching. Here are some experiences you might like to arrange:

1. Assume that intelligence in humans is stable and will not change as a result of external influences. Assume also that one or two of the items in the Simulated Intelligence Test Battery are valid measures of intelligence. Given these two assumptions, it is reasonable to expect that you could not *teach* someone to increase their performance on those tests. Your task would be to determine whether or not this is true. You might prepare several of the tracking pages with the same number of target stimuli and the same number of alternative stimuli as are in the tracking test in the Simulated Battery. In addition, prepare several practice pages using only numbers and not letters. After allowing your subject to practice with the numbers, check to see if his score with letters will change. You might also use this procedure with the auditory memory test. Practice could utilize either letters or words, whereas the test item uses numbers. Should the scores of the subject change from before to after practice, you will have to consider a number of implications: for instance, the test items are not a valid measure of intelligence; or intelligence is not fixed—it can change; or scores might be a function of anxiety level which decreases with exposure. Once you begin to believe one implication is more probable than another, you should consider what that means for your approach to learning and teaching.

2. Attempt to evaluate the effect the examiner has on the subject. One method of doing this would be to: A. Select a friend or close acquaintance for a subject (this is necessary so that you can explain afterward what you did); B. Have ready several forms of a certain test item like the maze, tracking, or auditory memory; C. Give the test item; D. Regardless of the score obtained by the subject, comment either positively or negatively about the score, for example, "I really can't believe you could do that poorly. Let's try it again!" or "Wow! What a score! Let's do that again!"; E. Consistently comment about subsequent scores and watch for deterioration or increase in performance level; F. Have another subject take the same number of tests, but make no comments. Make certain that you take the time to fully explain to the subject what you did during the experience. Try to discuss with him the evidence that you could or could not influence his test-taking behavior. Ask him for his perception of what was occurring. If the subject's scores do change in one direction or an-

other, consider the importance this has for your use of "intelligence" approaches to the process of classroom learning. Remember, your observations are subjective! They are or, at least, can be influenced by your own biases and expectations.

♦ SUGGESTED ADDITIONAL READINGS

For Basic Information About Intelligence

Anastasi, Anne. *Differential Psychology*. 3rd ed. New York: Macmillan, 1961.

Guilford, J. P. "Three Faces of Intellect." *American Psychologist* 14(1959):469–479.

Guilford, J. P. *The Nature of Human Intelligence*. New York: McGraw-Hill, 1967.

Robinson, H. B., and Robinson, Nancy. *The Mentally Retarded Child*, (Chapter One), New York: McGraw-Hill, 1965.

For More Detailed Information About Specific Theories of Intelligence

Guilford, J. P. *The Nature of Human Intelligence*. New York: McGraw-Hill, 1967.

Hunt, J. McV. *Intelligence and Experience*. New York: Ronald, 1961.

Vernon, P. E. *The Structure of Human Abilities*. 2nd ed. London: Methuen, 1961.

Wechsler, D. *Wechsler Intelligence Scale for Children: Manual*. New York: Psychological Corporation, 1949.

For Specific Studies Concerning Intelligence

Achenbach, T. M. "The Children's Associative Responding Test: A Possible Alternative to Group IQ Tests." *Journal of Educational Psychology* 61(1970): 340–348.

Denny, D. A. "Identification of Teacher-Classroom Variables Facilitating Pupil Creative Growth." *American Educational Research Journal* 5(1968):365–384.

Foulds, G. A. "Variations in the Intellectual Activities of Adults." *American Journal of Psychology* 62(1949):238–246.

Hinton, R. T., Jr. "The Role of the Basal Metabolic Rate in the Intelligence of Ninety Grade-School Children." *Journal of Educational Psychology* 30 (1936):309–314.

Kagan, J. S. et al, "How Much Can We Boost IQ and Scholastic Achievement?" *Harvard Educational Review* 39:(273–356).

Kreit, L. H. "The Effects of Test-Taking Practice on Pupil Test Performance." *American Educational Research Journal* 5(1968):616–625.

Page, J. D. "The Effect of Nursery School Attendance upon Subsequent IQ." *Journal of Psychology* 10(1940):221–230.

Rusch, R. R., Denny, D. A., & Ives, S. "Fostering Creativity in Sixth Grade." *Elementary School Journal* 65(1965):262–268.

Tyler, L. E. "The Stability of Patterns of Primary Mental Abilities Among Grade School Children." *Educational Psychology Measurement* 18(1958):769–774.

UNIT **3**

Social Perception

♦ BACKGROUND

> You will notice in this slide that the buildings are less elegant, less ornate, and smaller than the earlier slides.

> Look at this! What a great example of what I've been trying to make my students see!!

> I don't see how anyone could miss seeing the difference between a "b" and a "d."

The three statements above are examples of the way people talk about individual perceptions. An important part of teaching is the task of guiding students to the point of "seeing" new things. Teaching is perhaps just that— getting students to "see" new things, for example, seeing two different types of maple trees instead of just a "tree." But, there is another important aspect of "seeing" things; that is, seeing things as other people might see them. To many psychologists, especially developmental or child psychologists, that is an extremely important variable in the teaching and learning process. It is possible that individuals perceive things differently from one another, and if so, then a teacher might receive a great deal of help from knowing how perceptions differ. The experience aspect of this unit will allow you to observe perceptual differences between subjects, and the following background information should help make that experience meaningful.

What is the difference between "seeing, hearing, feeling," and "perceiving"?

To the layman there is usually not much difference between the terms, "seeing" and "perceiving." But, to the psychologist who concerns himself

57

with this approach to learning and teaching, there can be a great deal of difference. "Seeing" can be simply the phenomenon of energy inputs impinging on nerve cells and resulting in a change in electrochemical content. This part of human behavior is often called *sensation* and is different from the phenomenon called *perception*. Perception involves the activity that takes place somewhere further back in the nervous system. For example, suppose two individuals are positioned in identical locations in relation to a stimulus, and both individuals are exposed to exactly the same stimulus for the same amount of time. We can be reasonably certain that the energy input to the nerve cells of their eyes is precisely the same; yet the individuals can report that they "saw" different things, that is, they perceived different stimuli. At a more concrete level, consider the case of two people looking out at the horizon at night when a streak of lightning flashes. Both might claim that they "saw" something, that is, they can report a sensation. On the other hand, one might suggest that he perceived a rotating beacon while the other might claim that he perceived the sensation to be a flash like that from an explosion.

The perceptions of individuals are influenced by a great many different variables. The one variable with which this unit is concerned is of a social nature.

What is meant by "social perception"?

Whereas sensations are influenced in a large part by the physical energy present, perceptions can be influenced by such things as the relationships between individuals and the values placed on these relationships. Relationships such as these can be called "social." Therefore, perceptions which are a part of the "social milieu" are social perceptions. Hence, comes the study of social perception, or stated another way, the study of man's perceptions as they relate to social factors.

An example of social perceptions operating is the rather commonplace instance of two people from different socio-economic groups seeing the same event and evaluating it in different ways. This is a common theme for fiction writers to use: the defendant is a "hoodlum" from a minority-group-ghetto area; one witness to the crime is an upper-middle-class business man who sees the defendant as vicious, intoxicated, addicted, ruthless, etc.; while the other witness from a background similar to the "hoodlum" sees the defendant as frightened, reluctant, innocent, etc. Assuming that both witnesses experienced similar sensations, it appears that their final perceptions were influenced by factors which were social rather than physical.

What might a psychologist look for in social perception research?

Studies of social perception often concentrate on answering the question, What aspects of the physical stimulus are critical to differences in perception? Essentially, they are looking for the cues which people use to make perceptual judgments. For instance, a researcher might look for the critical facial features which are used by people to judge whether the face is friendly, agreeable, angry, and so on. To do this he might present to a subject five pictures which are exactly identical except for measured changes in the curvature of the mouth. Picture number one might have the mouth curving upward at the corners, whereas picture number five could have the mouth curving slightly downward. If subjects consistently perceive the picture with the upward curving mouth as being friendly and the downward curving mouth as being unfriendly, then the researcher can begin to consider the position of the mouth as a significant cue to perception of friendliness.

An important difference should be noted between the two examples of social perception above. In the example of the witnesses and the defendant, the inital differences were within the subjects—they supposedly saw the same thing; yet perceptions differed. In the second example of the facial features research, the initial differences were in the stimuli present, not in the subjects. So, at least two factors can influence social perception; individual differences in the subject and differences in the physical stimuli. Psychological researchers often consider a third variable which can influence perception; the amount of information the perceiver has about the stimuli being viewed. In a sense, this is much like individual differences. For example, a subject might have the information that a stumbling derelict has a disease of the central nervous system and perceive the derelict's condition as neutral or distressing, whereas without the information he would perceive the same scene as shameful or disgraceful.

In the experience part of this unit you will be considering three different variables in social perception; the differences between the subjects, the differences between stimuli presented, and the differences in information available to the subject.

How is "social perception" important to the teacher?

Psychologists who have stressed the social perception approach to learning and teaching believe that the teacher can and should consider the perceptions of students when interacting with them in a classroom. For example, if elementary age children perceive certain situations in a way that is different from adults, then the adult teacher should have some knowledge of the difference. Such knowledge would help the teacher to predict the responses of children given certain situations, and would also provide an "entering behavior" level which could be used to measure change in perception over a period of time. In addition, if an adult teacher assumed that the students perceived things in exactly the way he did, then he might progress to more advanced levels based on that earlier assumed perception. If the students did not share the earlier perception, then the advanced work might be difficult to comprehend. Thus, "understanding" the perceptions of others could be an important attribute for a teacher to possess.

The experience portion of this unit will help you decide whether or not the perceptions of others are important to the teacher. You have sufficient background information at this point to engage in an experience much like one pursued by psychologists concerned with the area of social perception.

♦ AN EXPERIENCE

Before stating the Experience Objectives it would be well to have a short explanation of the nature of the experience. You will note that in the materials section of this unit are some stick-figure pictures which are called "plates." There are sixteen of those plates. The plates will be the stimuli which you will present to subjects. As mentioned in the background material, the three variables which will be manipulated are individual differences, differences in physical stimuli, and differences in amount of information about the plates. Here is how you will manipulate the three variables:

Individual differences: You are to select five or more subjects who differ in identifiable ways such as sex, age, or occupation. You will show them the pictures and score their responses. The important data you will be looking at on this level will be the *differences between subjects*, that is, you will compare the responses of Subject 1 to Subject 2 for the same plates.

Differences in physical stimuli: The plates are designed so that they differ in certain specified ways. The major consistent difference between the plates is that some have one figure's face shaded and the other figure's face is not shaded. (Each plate has two figures on it.) Other plates have both figures not shaded. In addition to shading you should note that the plates are paired, that is, Plate 1 and Plate 8 have the same figures in the same positions, but Plate 1 has two unshaded while Plate 8 has one shaded figure and one unshaded figure. There are also differences in facial expressions between paired plates. The chart in Figure 3.1 explains which plates are paired and the differences between paired plates. In order to evaluate the effect of differences in physical stimuli, you will look at the differences in responses to each of the paired plates *within subjects*. For example, if the same subject judges Plate 1 differently from Plate 8, then, perhaps, the change can be attributed to the difference in physical features between the two plates.

Differences in amount of information about the plates: The procedure called for in this experience suggests that you show the plates to each subject twice. The first time through the plates you do not give them any information about the figures on the plates. The second time through, you tell the subject that one of the figures is a teacher. The subject must decide which figure is the teacher. Since you, the experimenter, will not tell the subject anything about the other (non-teacher) figure, we assume that the subject must make his own identification of that figure. In this instance you will evaluate the data to find *within subject differences* between the first time through the plates and the second time through when one figure was a teacher. If dif-

Paired Plates	Differences Between Plates
1 and 8	Plate 1—both figures unshaded, Plate 8—left figure shaded with facial features different
2 and 12	Plate 2—left figure shaded, Plate 12—both figures unshaded with facial features different
3 and 15	Plate 3—both figures unshaded, Plate 15—left figure shaded with facial features different on both figures
4 and 10	Plate 4—right figure shaded, Plate 10—both figures unshaded
5 and 9	Plate 5—both figures unshaded, Plate 9—upper figure shaded
6 and 14	Plate 6—left figure shaded, Plate 14—both figures unshaded with right figure facial features different
7 and 13	Plate 7—both figures unshaded, Plate 13—right figure shaded with facial features different
11 and 16	Plate 11—right figure shaded, Plate 16—both figures unshaded

Figure 3.1 Table identifying paired plates and differences between pairs.

ferences do occur, say for instance, between Plate 1 the first time and Plate 1 the second time, you should begin to consider the added information as a variable in perception.

In the paragraphs above we have referred to the "responses of the subjects." This implies that you as the experimenter will ask the subject to respond to the plates in some manner. If you leave the choice of response open to the subject, you might get such diversified responses that comparison would be difficult if not impossible. In order to avoid confusion of that sort, it is suggested that you ask the subject to look at the plate and quickly tell you whether he perceives it to be an instance of "aggression," "affection," or "neutral." So the differences you will be looking for will be from "aggression to affection," neutral to aggression," etc.

This experience tends to be a little more complex than those associated with Units 1 and 2, but the Experience Objectives, The Suggested Procedures, and the guideline sheets which follow should help you complete the experience.

Experience Objectives

1. You should administer the Social Perception Experience Plate Set (using the prescribed procedure) to five subjects.
2. You should enter the data from each subject on the proper Data Table.
3. You should prepare a summary description of the experience.

Suggested Procedure for Achieving the Experience Objectives

1. Read the sheet labeled, "Directions for the Experimenter." The experimenter is the person conducting the experience. Also read over the Data Tables For The First and Second Sequence of Plates. Look through the Plate Set, using the Data Table to identify those plates which are paired. Coordinate the Subject Response Sheet with the Directions for the Experimenter so that you are certain of the procedure once you confront a subject.
2. Identify a variable which you can use to discriminate subjects from each other. If you choose a variable with only two categories like sex, then find two subjects from each category who will volunteer, i.e., two males and two females. If you use a variable like annual family income which could have more than two categories, then you might use only one subject per category and, perhaps, need more than five subjects. Make some attempt to control other variables like age, sex (if it is not the variable being manipulated), marital status, etc.
3. Conduct the experience with the subjects chosen. (Read the directions for the first sequence of plates, display those plates and score the subject's responses for that sequence. Read the directions for the second sequence of plates. Display and score the subject's responses for that sequence. Point out to the subject differences between subjects and/or differences in a single subject's responses to paired plates. Interview the subject using the questions at the bottom of each Subject Response Sheet.)
4. Transfer your data from the Subject Response Sheets to the Data Tables.

5. Use the Experience Summary Guidelines Sheet to prepare a description of your experience.

Progress Chart

Activity	Check each space when completed.
1. All relevant material read	_____
2. Between subjects variable selected	_____
3. Experience conducted: Subject 1	_____
4. Experience conducted: Subject 2	_____
5. Experience conducted: Subject 3	_____
6. Experience conducted: Subject 4	_____
7. Experience conducted: Subject 5	_____
8. Data transferred to Data Tables	_____
9. Summary report prepared	_____

DIRECTIONS FOR THE EXPERIMENTER

1. Be certain that you have a clock with a sweep second hand, a pencil, an answer sheet, and the Plate Set ready when you begin the experience with the subject.

2. Place the Plate Set in front of the subject and ask him not to turn any pages until directed to do so.

3. Read the following directions to the subject for Plates 1–16 (the first sequence).

> The booklet which I have placed in front of you contains pictures which you will be permitted to look at briefly. When you look at each picture I want you to tell me whether you perceive "Aggression," "Affection," or "Neutral" (pause). You are to say one of those words to indicate your choice—"Aggression," "Affection," or "Neutral." You will have only a brief time to look at the picture so make your choice quickly. When I say "turn" you are to turn to the next picture. Please do not turn to the next picture before I say "turn" but you must turn the page as soon as I say "turn." Do you have any questions?

4. If the subject does ask questions, try to answer them by rereading the directions. Give as little additional information as possible. If there are no questions, then you should say, "Ready . . . Begin." As soon as the subject responds to a plate, you should mark his choice on the SUBJECT RESPONSE SHEET and immediately say "turn." Do not give the subject any longer than ten (10) seconds on any plate.

5. When the subject finishes the first sequence of plates, you should read the following directions for Plates 17–32:

> You are to look at the plates again, but in this sequence you are to assume that one of the figures is a teacher. I will not tell you which one nor will I tell you what the other figure is. Respond by saying either "Aggression," or "Affection," or "Neutral." Are there any questions?

6. Record the subject's responses for Plates 17–32 just as you did for Plates 1–16.

No._____

Subject Response Sheet

1.	AG	N	AF	17.	AG	N	AF
2.	AG	N	AF	18.	AG	N	AF
3.	AG	N	AF	19.	AG	N	AF
4.	AG	N	AF	20.	AG	N	AF
5.	AG	N	AF	21.	AG	N	AF
6.	AG	N	AF	22.	AG	N	AF
7.	AG	N	AF	23.	AG	N	AF
8.	AG	N	AF	24.	AG	N	AF
9.	AG	N	AF	25.	AG	N	AF
10.	AG	N	AF	26.	AG	N	AF
11.	AG	N	AF	27.	AG	N	AF
12.	AG	N	AF	28.	AG	N	AF
13.	AG	N	AF	29.	AG	N	AF
14.	AG	N	AF	30.	AG	N	AF
15.	AG	N	AF	31.	AG	N	AF
16.	AG	N	AF	32.	AG	N	AF

After the subject has completed the first and second sequence with the Plate Set, you should ask him the following questions:

1. Did you notice any differences between the pictures you saw? If so, what were the differences?

2. Did you change your response from one picture to another? If so, why? Why did you perceive one as being different from another?

3. Did you identify one figure as a teacher? If so, what was the basis for your choice? What was the other figure in most cases?

No._____

Subject Response Sheet

1.	AG	N	AF	17.	AG	N	AF
2.	AG	N	AF	18.	AG	N	AF
3.	AG	N	AF	19.	AG	N	AF
4.	AG	N	AF	20.	AG	N	AF
5.	AG	N	AF	21.	AG	N	AF
6.	AG	N	AF	22.	AG	N	AF
7.	AG	N	AF	23.	AG	N	AF
8.	AG	N	AF	24.	AG	N	AF
9.	AG	N	AF	25.	AG	N	AF
10.	AG	N	AF	26.	AG	N	AF
11.	AG	N	AF	27.	AG	N	AF
12.	AG	N	AF	28.	AG	N	AF
13.	AG	N	AF	29.	AG	N	AF
14.	AG	N	AF	30.	AG	N	AF
15.	AG	N	AF	31.	AG	N	AF
16.	AG	N	AF	32.	AG	N	AF

After the subject has completed the first and second sequence with the Plate Set, you should ask him the following questions:

1. Did you notice any differences between the pictures you saw? If so, what were the differences?

2. Did you change your response from one picture to another? If so, why? Why did you perceive one as being different from another?

3. Did you identify one figure as a teacher? If so, what was the basis for your choice? What was the other figure in most cases?

No._____

Subject Response Sheet

1.	AG	N	AF		17.	AG	N	AF
2.	AG	N	AF		18.	AG	N	AF
3.	AG	N	AF		19.	AG	N	AF
4.	AG	N	AF		20.	AG	N	AF
5.	AG	N	AF		21.	AG	N	AF
6.	AG	N	AF		22.	AG	N	AF
7.	AG	N	AF		23.	AG	N	AF
8.	AG	N	AF		24.	AG	N	AF
9.	AG	N	AF		25.	AG	N	AF
10.	AG	N	AF		26.	AG	N	AF
11.	AG	N	AF		27.	AG	N	AF
12.	AG	N	AF		28.	AG	N	AF
13.	AG	N	AF		29.	AG	N	AF
14.	AG	N	AF		30.	AG	N	AF
15.	AG	N	AF		31.	AG	N	AF
16.	AG	N	AF		32.	AG	N	AF

After the subject has completed the first and second sequence with the Plate Set, you should ask him the following questions:

1. Did you notice any differences between the pictures you saw? If so, what were the differences?

2. Did you change your response from one picture to another? If so, why? Why did you perceive one as being different from another?

3. Did you identify one figure as a teacher? If so, what was the basis for your choice? What was the other figure in most cases?

No._____

Subject Response Sheet

1.	AG	N	AF		17.	AG	N	AF
2.	AG	N	AF		18.	AG	N	AF
3.	AG	N	∧F		19.	AG	N	AF
4.	AG	N	AF		20.	AG	N	AF
5.	AG	N	AF		21.	AG	N	AF
6.	AG	N	AF		22.	AG	N	AF
7.	AG	N	AF		23.	AG	N	AF
8.	AG	N	AF		24.	AG	N	AF
9.	AG	N	AF		25.	AG	N	AF
10.	AG	N	AF		26.	AG	N	AF
11.	AG	N	AF		27.	AG	N	AF
12.	AG	N	AF		28.	AG	N	AF
13.	AG	N	AF		29.	AG	N	AF
14.	AG	N	AF		30.	AG	N	AF
15.	AG	N	AF		31.	AG	N	AF
16.	AG	N	AF		32.	AG	N	AF

After the subject has completed the first and second sequence with the Plate Set, you should ask him the following questions:

1. Did you notice any differences between the pictures you saw? If so, what were the differences?

2. Did you change your response from one picture to another? If so, why? Why did you perceive one as being different from another?

3. Did you identify one figure as a teacher? If so, what was the basis for your choice? What was the other figure in most cases?

No._____

Subject Response Sheet

1.	AG	N	AF		17.	AG	N	AF
2.	AG	N	AF		18.	AG	N	AF
3.	AG	N	AF		19.	AG	N	AF
4.	AG	N	AF		20.	AG	N	AF
5.	AG	N	AF		21.	AG	N	AF
6.	AG	N	AF		22.	AG	N	AF
7.	AG	N	AF		23.	AG	N	AF
8.	AG	N	AF		24.	AG	N	AF
9.	AG	N	AF		25.	AG	N	AF
10.	AG	N	AF		26.	AG	N	AF
11.	AG	N	AF		27.	AG	N	AF
12.	AG	N	AF		28.	AG	N	AF
13.	AG	N	AF		29.	AG	N	AF
14.	AG	N	AF		30.	AG	N	AF
15.	AG	N	AF		31.	AG	N	AF
16.	AG	N	AF		32.	AG	N	AF

After the subject has completed the first and second sequence with the Plate Set, you should ask him the following questions:

1. Did you notice any differences between the pictures you saw? If so, what were the differences?

2. Did you change your response from one picture to another? If so, why? Why did you perceive one as being different from another?

3. Did you identify one figure as a teacher? If so, what was the basis for your choice? What was the other figure in most cases?

♦ SOCIAL PERCEPTION EXPERIENCE
PLATE SET

Plate 1 (17)

Plate 2 (18)

Plate 3 (19)

Plate 4 (20)

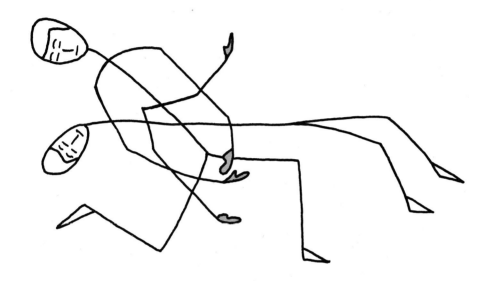

Plate 5 (21)

Plate 6 (22)

Plate 7 (23)

Plate 8 (24)

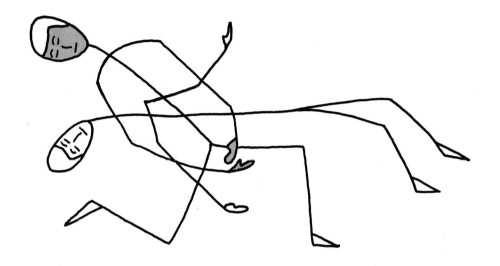

Plate 9 (25)

Plate 10 (26)

Plate 11 (27)

91

Plate 12 (28)

Plate 13 (29)

Plate 14 (30)

97

Plate 15 (31)

Plate 16 (32)

Data Table for First Sequence of Plates

(Subject has no information about the figures in the Plates.)

DIRECTION OF CHANGE					
Subjects					
Plates	1	2	3	4	5
1–8					
2–12					
3–15					
4–10					
5–9					
6–14					
7–13					
11–16					

Directions for completing the Data Table: For each subject use the follow-ing symbols to indicate change from one plate to another; Ag for aggression, Af for affection, N for neutral, X for no change. If Subject 1 judged Plate 1 to be affection and Plate 8 to be neutral, then the experimenter would enter the symbols Af→N in the space below Subject 1 on the table and to the right of the 1–8 Plates.

Data Table for Comparing the First and Second Sequence of Plates

DIRECTION OF CHANGE					
Subjects					
Plates	1	2	3	4	5
1–17					
2–18					
3–19					
4–20					
5–21					
6–22					
7–23					
8–24					
9–25					
10–26					
11–27					
12–28					
13–29					
14–30					
15–31					
16–32					

Directions for completing the Data Table: This table should show the changes made by each subject between the first sequence of plates (1–16) and the second (17–32) when one of the figures was labeled a "teacher." Use the following symbols to indicate change from one plate to another; Ag for aggression, Af for affection, N for neutral, X for no change. For example, if Subject 1 judged Plate 1 to be affection and Plate 17 to be neutral, then the symbols, Af→N, should appear below Subject 1 on the table and to the right of the 1–17 Plates.

Experience Summary Guidelines Sheet

You should use the data from the Data Tables and from the questions you asked the subjects to prepare a summary report of your experience.

1. Were trends evident from the Data Tables? What direction? What variables might influence those trends?

2. How did your subjects differ from one another? (Another way of phrasing this question is "What was the variable used to separate individuals for between subjects evaluation?") Did this variable turn out to be one which influenced "between subject differences?"

3. Can you identify a predominant change from the first to the second sequence?

4. When you questioned the subjects after the experience, what were some of the differences which they perceived in the plates?

5. Evaluate the reasons your subjects gave for changing responses from one plate to another, especially from one member of a pair to the other member. Do you agree that the reason given is probably the "true" cause? Why?

6. Identify the trends, changes, differences, comments, etc. which seem to have some relevance to teaching and learning. Why are they relevant? What do they imply?

7. Give an example of how you would use the information gained from this unit.

♦ SUMMARY

In the background portion of this unit three major questions were dealt with: first, What is the difference between common terms like "seeing" and the less common term "perceiving?"; second, What is social perception?; third, How is social perception important to a teacher? In addition, examples were given of the various ways psychologists research social perception, and the variables which they manipulate during the research. Three major variables were identified; (1) The differences between individuals, (2) The differences in physical stimuli, (3) The differences in information about the physical stimuli.

The experience aspect of this unit affords the reader the opportunity to investigate the three major variables identified above. Sixteen pictures called plates were provided as stimuli for the experience. Each plate had two stick figures drawn on it, and the plates were paired so that one plate of a pair differed in some specified way from the other member of the pair. The major differences built into the plates were shading on one figure on one plate and not on the other, and minute differences in facial expression, usually a change in mouth shape. The suggested procedure was to ask five subjects to describe their perceptions of the scenes on the plates as either aggression, affection or neutral. Each subject was to go through the plates twice, the second time having the information that one of the figures was a teacher. The data collected were to be evaluated in terms of between subject differences and within subject changes given differences in stimuli and differences in information. It was suggested that the reader try to draw some conclusions or implications from the limited data collected.

Since the amount of data collected was limited, it is difficult to come to well-supported conclusions or identify concrete implications. During the early field testing of this experience, the accusation was repeatedly raised that even if the one figure of the pair was called "shaded," what was *really* meant was black, or "colored." This is a difficult accusation to deny, and there seems to be little reason for denial. If the experimenter or the subjects perceived the shaded figure as black, or red, or colored, or whatever, then *that* is a good example of individual perception in operation. If the experimenter was careful not to refer to the figure as anything but simply "shaded," then, it seems reasonable to assume that the subject who referred to the same figure as "black" did so because he perceived it that way. In at least one of the pilot studies with the plates, it was found that young children did not perceive the shaded figures as black. Some referred to them as dark, but not specifically black. If you showed the plates to young children and to adults, what did you find? Did your results coincide with the pilot work described above? Can you assume that adults perceive things differently from children?

Did you find any evidence in your data to show that individual perceptions might be different in spite of stimulus similarity? What implications can you offer in regard to your findings? If two different students perceived the same scene in two different ways, does that finding suggest specific actions a teacher should take? For example, suppose you found that one subject did not perceive any of the plates as "affection" in the second sequence when one figure was a teacher, but previously perceived several as affection. Can you infer from this data that the subject has difficulty perceiving a teacher as being affectionate? If you do make such an inference, can you speculate on what teachers should do with this subject that would be different from any other subject?

If social perception has any relationship to the teaching/learning process, then the principles underlying that relationship should be specified. It is only when those principles are clearly stated that teachers can behave in a specified, positive manner and evaluate the effects of their behavior. Can you state a principle arising from the experience in this unit? Does that principle prescribe what the teacher can or should do given certain conditions. Or does it simply explain a "cause and effect" relationship that will better permit the teacher to understand a child. An example of the point toward which this discussion is moving would be a case where someone stated the principle, "Adults are more likely than children to perceive the plates with shaded figures as aggressive." A principle such as that simply describes a condition which exists. It does not state why it happens. Suppose the principle was extended to include the phrase, "because adults have had more experience with non-white people and see them as typically aggressive." True or not, the principle still only describes what happens and infers a causation for that happening. The critical question still remains, What does the teacher do with this information? There are no easy or ready answers for that question. Psychology has not progressed to the point where it is possible to say that Principle X applies in Z situation, so therefore, Behavior A is appropriate for the teacher. The actions taken by a teacher in relation to information of the type given above are largely of an individual, experiential, or logical nature rather than of a scientific, empirical nature. So, the adoption of a social perceptual approach to learning and teaching and the behaviors which result from that adoption will require a great deal of questioning and critical analysis on your part.

The Suggested Additional Activities and Readings which follow should provide further information to you regarding the social perception approach to learning and teaching.

♦ SUGGESTED ADDITIONAL ACTIVITIES

1. Consider the question as to whether or not the limited data collected during the normal experience in this unit is actually representative of a larger population. An activity which would offer the answer to that question would be to extend the experience to more than just five people. If you followed the exact same procedure with thirty or more people, then you could begin to identify reliable differences between people or consistent changes in perception. The tables in Figures 3.2 and 3.3 represent data collected from eighty-three college sophomores, juniors, and seniors. How much is your data like that in the tables? Do differences or changes appear on the same plates? Can you reach any different conclusions with more data than you could with the five subjects?

2. It is the author's opinion that if one wishes to become a teacher, then you could have no better experience than to actually interact with students at every level of education. The plates used in this experience provide a vehicle for talking with children, experiencing the difficulties of giving instructions, recognizing the limitations of verbal communication in the early grades—the list is endless. Select an elementary and secondary school that you can get to readily. Arrange for a space (through the principal) where you can work with one student at a time. Secure the permission of the teachers to use two students from each grade as subjects. At the end of your experience you will have had the opportunity of interacting with twenty-six students at thirteen different age levels. The similarities and differences you will perceive will be more than worth the time spent. Of course, you will have to alter the procedure for younger children inasmuch as many students from the first through the sixth grade will not comprehend the terms, aggression, affection, and neutral. You might simply ask students to tell you what they think is happening in the pictures. You very well might be able to translate their descriptions into the terms used in the earlier experience.

3. Aggression, affection, and neutral are not the only terms which can be used to determine the perceptions of subjects, and the procedure can be changed along with the words. For instance the subject could be presented with 32 scales (three inch lines) with "friendly" at one end and "unfriendly" at another. The directions would be "Place an 'X' at the point on the scale corresponding to your perception of the scene on the plate."

Plates	Direction of Change
1–8	X (N)
2–12	Ag→N/Af
3–15	Af→N/Ag
4–10	X (Af)
5–9	X (Af)
6–14	X (N)
7–13	X (Ag)
11–16	X (N)

Af = Affection
Ag = Aggression
N = Neutral
X = No Change
/ = Split in direction of change
→ = Direction of change
( ) = Predominant perceptual term selected

Figure 3.2 Summary data from eighty-three college students who were Subjects in Unit Three Experience—First sequence (Plates 1–16).

Plates	Direction of Change
1–17	X (N)
2–18	Ag→Af
3–19	X (Af)
4–20	X (Af)
5–21	X (Af)
6–22	N→Af
7–23	X (Ag)
8–24	N→Ag
9–25	X (Af)
10–26	X (Af)
11–27	X (N)
12–28	X (Af = N = Ag)
13–29	Ag→Af
14–30	X (N)
15–31	X (Af)
16–32	X (N)

Af = Affection
Ag = Aggression
N = Neutral
X = No change
→ = Direction of change
( ) = Predominant perceptual term selected

Figure 3.3 Summary data from eighty-three college students who were Subjects in Unit Three Experience—Second Sequence (Plates 17–32).

♦ SUGGESTED ADDITIONAL READINGS

For Basic Information on Perception and Social Perception

Freedman, J. L.; Carlsmith, J. M.; and Sears, D. O. *Social Psychology* (especially Chapter Two, Person Perception). Englewood Cliffs, N.J.: Prentice-Hall, 1970.

Hochberg, J. E. *Perception.* Englewood Cliffs, N.J.: Prentice-Hall, 1964.

For More Advanced Information

Hastorf, A. H.; Schneider, D.; and Polefka, J. *Person Perception,* Reading, Mass.: Addison-Wesley, 1970.

Tagiuri, R., and Petrullo, L. *Person Perception and Interpersonal Behavior.* Stanford: Stanford University Press, 1958.

For Information Regarding Specific Studies

Beardslee, D. C., and Wertheimer, M. *Readings in Perception.* Princeton, N.J.: Van Nostrand, 1958.

Rist, R. C. "Student Social Class and Teacher Expectations: The Self-Fulfilling Prophecy in Ghetto Education." *Harvard Educational Review* 40(1970): 411–451.

Toch, H., and Smith, H. C. *Social Perception.* Princeton, N.J.: Van Nostrand, 1968. (This book contains twenty-five specific articles related to social perception.)

UNIT 4

Conceptual Processes

♦ BACKGROUND

Intellectual growth and development for a human being includes a variety of steps and processes, and foremost among these is the process which some psychologists have called "conceptualization." This particular phenomenon can come under other titles like "concept attainment" or "concept learning," and some psychologists make distinctions between the terms. On the whole, however, conceptual processes usually are those thought patterns by which humans arrive at the point of putting like things in categories. For the teacher or any other individual who is concerned with learning and education, knowledge of conceptual processes could offer tremendous insight into the problems and mistakes of the learner. For example, just how does a young child acquire the concepts of male and female? Surely, very few children sit down with parents and listen to a carefully organized description of the characteristics of each sex which differentiate them. It is probably more often the case that they are exposed to examples of the two concepts and at the same time receive some type of confirmation about the nature of the exposure. It is fairly easy to see that with a multiple exposure procedure, a number of variables will influence the degree to which the concept is attained, the rate and ease with which it is attained, and the incorrect notions established about the concept.

The background portion of this unit will begin with a discussion of how psychologists have approached the problem of investigating the conceptual processes and progress to familiarize you with the terms and "concepts" involved.

How is "categorization" related to conceptualization?

A number of psychologists have approached the study of the conceptual processes by viewing them as the process by which people categorize objects, experiences, sounds, etc. around them. This means that a concept is something which can be reliably placed in a group with other things like it. The members of that group have characteristics in common which make them a part of that concept. For example, the concept, "sky," has certain characteristics like clouds, blueness, vastness, and position which allow a person to categorize it from a mountain top, an ocean liner, a prairie field, a cave mouth, through a "skylight" or on a movie screen. On the other hand a mountain range is not part of that sky, although it has height, nor is a lake although it is blue, nor is a farm field although it is vast; therefore, none of these things are instances of the concept. To a child, however, any one of the above mentioned objects could be considered part of the concept, sky, until information to the contrary becomes available.

Categorization appears to be a process by which we place things in classes. This implies that initially an array of things might be all the same to the observer. A case in point is the child who is viewing "people." They are all the same until he can classify "people" as "male" and "female." At the same time he is acquiring the skill to classify "people" into two categories, he is also attaining the concepts, "male" and "female."

What are positive and negative instances of a concept?

Positive instances of a concept are simply those situations in which a correct example of the concept is present. They are sometimes called positive examples. A positive example of the concept, boat, could be a picture of a boat, an actual boat, or some other situation in which a correct example of a boat was present. In a negative instance the example present in the situation is not a member of the group of things which depict the concept being considered. For example, a goat is a negative instance when the concept, cow, is being considered.

What is a "concept universe"?

The sum total of different things that make up a concept is usually referred to as the "universe of things in the concept." For example, holstein and black angus cows are part of the universe of things in the concept, cows, but certainly, not the complete list of things in the concept. Your right and left hands do make up the total universe of things in the concept, "my hands."

What are the "critical attributes" of a concept?

The properties of a concept which allow a person to distinguish it from other concepts are the critical attributes of a concept. The denseness of wood is one of its properties which distinguishes it from plastic or metal. Size, shape, and color are all critical attributes of a cow, while the fact that it is alive might not be a critical attribute if the total universe of things being considered are all animate. The fact that a dog has four legs is not critical to the identification of the concept, dog, if the negative examples present also have four legs like the concepts, cat, horse, sheep, and goat.

Critical attributes are called "relevant dimensions" by some psychologists. The characteristics of a concept which are not critical to its identification among other concepts are sometimes called "irrelevant dimensions." During the process of conceptualization, a person will often attend to irrelevant dimensions and formulate an incorrect notion of the concept in question. An example of this situation might be the case where initial exposures to poetry lead one to believe that the concept, poetry, must have lines of print which are shorter than a normal line of print. Literature instructors would probably say that the length of the line of print is irrelevant to the concept, poetry, therefore, it becomes an irrelevant dimension.

What problems do psychologists encounter when investigating the conceptual processes?

Now that you are familiar with the terms associated with the study of the conceptual processes, let us take a look at the manner in which they are used. First, consider the problem of how to study what someone is thinking. Of course, it can't be done with absolute certainty, and *that* is a problem for psychologists who wish to scientifically study the ways people go about establishing concepts. For instance, just because we use the word, "sky," to denote a particular phenomenon in our environment, it is not necessary for the word, "sky," to be associated with the concept in order for the concept to be attained. Let's clarify that a little—a person can be exposed to positive and negative examples of a concept and begin to distinguish the critical attributes of the concept without naming the concept. In other words, the process is a cognitive or mental one which the psychologist cannot directly observe. It, therefore, becomes necessary for him to ask for some external form of behavior which he can observe and measure. An external form of behavior often used is the verbal report. Verbal reports can be prompted by a question like, What do you *think* the concept is? Another form of behavior which the psychologist can observe is that of having the subject identify whether or not a specific instance is a positive or negative example. From an accurate description or from a set of correctly identified examples the psychologist can infer that the person *knows* the concept. Or another way of stating it is that the person has gone through the necessary mental processes to attain the correct concept. So, we can say that conceptual processes are essentially mental or thought processes, and the psychologist can investigate them by making inferences based on observable behavior.

Now, the problem of what concepts to use in research must be considered. There are at least two major obstacles to using concepts which are common to our everyday experience: First, the researcher has no control over the subject's past experience with the concept, therefore, prior learning can cast doubt on the findings secured from laboratory research; and second, most common, everyday concepts have large numbers of positive examples in their universes, thereby making the laboratory exercise and materials cumbersome and lengthy. To overcome these two problems psychologists have developed artificial concepts with a limited number of examples in the total universe. For example, look at the Total Figures Chart in this unit. On that chart you will find five visual figures which can take six different forms. This gives a universe of thirty different figures. The psychologist can arbitrarily say that the concept to be attained or learned by the subject includes those figures with A, B, and C attributes or dimensions. Another way of saying this is that A, B, and C are the relevant dimensions of the concept while D, E, F, and all the rest are irrelevant dimensions. For example, the concept to be attained by the subject could be those figures which have only three sides and two circles within the figure. On the Total Figures Chart the positive examples of that concept would be figures 5C and 6C. With two tools, an observable subject behavior, and a universe of examples, plus a few questions, the psychologist can begin studying the multitude of variables associated with conceptual processes.

Give an example of how psychologists have approached the problem of investigating the conceptual processes.

The aim of this book is to introduce the reader to an area within psychology and provide a concrete example of work done in that area; so the reader should realize that the single example briefly described below does not represent all of the work done on conceptual processes. A description or even a summary of the other work done is not within the domain of this book, but the interested reader can pursue the topic further by consulting the literature listed in the Suggested Additional Readings list.

Jerome Bruner, Jacqueline Goodnow, and George Austin collaborated on a book entitled, *A Study of Thinking*,[1] which describes the many studies they supervised in the area of conceptual processes. In their investigations they employed a number of different methods of presenting visual figures and sampling the subject's mental processes. Foremost in their work was the analysis of the strategies used by their subjects to learn or attain concepts. A simplified sample of how these psychologists would operate follows: A subject was shown positive and negative examples of a concept one at a time, and after each exposure the experimenter would tell the subject whether the example was positive or negative. The first example was always positive. After each example the experimenter would ask the subject to state an hypothesis regarding the nature of the concept. In this manner the experimenter could follow the progress of the subject and from his verbal reports infer the strategy used by the subject. The types of observations important in such a procedure would be instances in which the subject altered his hypothesis in two different ways when the information in the example only justified a single alteration. Or, perhaps, the subject would not efficiently use the information in negative examples and as a result not attain the concept in the minimum time possible. The experience in this unit is closely related to the work done by Bruner et al; so let us assume that you will gain more from a concrete experience than from the author's description of such an experience. Without further delay let us consider the experience in this unit.

1. J. S. Bruner, Jacqueline J. Goodnow, and G. A. Austin, *A Study of Thinking* (New York: Wiley and Sons, 1956).

♦ AN EXPERIENCE

How is the experience in this unit related to psychological studies of the conceptual processes?

There are two exercises in the experience aspect of this unit. In the first you will present positive and negative examples of a concept to the subject and ask him to tell you what he thinks the concept is. By following his progress in this manner, you can begin to recognize how incorrect conceptualizations are formed, how both negative and positive examples can act to confirm incorrect conceptualizations, and how attention to certain attributes and not others can reduce the efficiency of concept formation processes. The experience you will have is much like those encountered in the lab by psychologists; so in order to increase applicability you will be encouraged to relate your findings to a real-life situation encountered by a child.

In the second exercise you will have a chance to evaluate the effects of risk-taking on the conceptual processes and their efficiency. You will progress in the same manner as in the first exercise, however, this time you will not ask the subject to describe his hypotheses about the concept. He is to collect information from each example and revise his thinking until he is sure that he can identify the concept in question. At that point he can "take a chance" at identifying the next five examples without your help. Two mistakes and he loses the exercise. There is a point at which you as the experimenter will know that enough examples have been given for a correct identification. With this information in mind you will be concerned with questions such as: Can the subject use the information in each example so as to attain the concept in the minimal amount of exposures? Will he seek additional examples even after he "has" the concept in order to verify his ideas? Just how efficient will he be? What dimensions will he attend to? Can you be sure that you know what the possible irrelevant dimensions are? The Summary and Report Guidelines Sheets for the two exercises will help you evaluate the experiences. The specific Experience Objectives are as follows:

Experience Objectives

1. You should locate a subject who will agree to spend a minimum of 30 minutes with you on a concept learning task.
2. You should conduct Exercises A and B with the subject and during the exercise record the behaviors of the subject as specified in the Directions and Response Sheets.

3. You should complete the Summary and Report Guidelines Sheets for both exercises.

4. You should locate a second subject and complete Experience Objectives 2 and 3 with the second subject.

Suggested Procedure for Achieving the Experience Objectives

1. Read quickly through the Directions and Response Sheets for Exercise A, and relate the figures in the Picture Set with the Directions.

2. Read quickly through the Summary and Report Guidelines Sheets for Exercise A in order to anticipate what you should look for in the Exercise.

3. Read quickly through the Directions and Response Sheets for Exercise B, and relate the figures in the Picture Set with the Directions.

4. Read quickly through the Summary and Report Guidelines Sheets for Exercise B in order to anticipate what you should look for in that Exercise.

5. Conduct Exercises A and B with your first subject.

6. Report the results of the Exercises with the first subject using the space available on the Summary and Report Guidelines Sheets.

7. Read the Summary for this unit.

8. Conduct Exercises A and B with your second subject.

9. Report the results of the Exercises with the second subject using the remaining space available on the Summary and Report Guidelines Sheets.

10. Scan the Summary for this unit a second time.

Progress Chart

	Activity	Check each space when completed.
1.	Read Directions and Response Sheets for Exercise A	_____
2.	Relate figures to Exercise A Directions	_____
3.	Read Exercise A Summary and Report Guidelines Sheets	_____
4.	Read Directions and Response Sheets for Exercise B	_____
5.	Relate figures to Exercise B Directions	_____
6.	Read Exercise B Summary and Report Guidelines Sheets	_____
7.	Exercises A and B completed with first subject	_____
8.	Report results with first subject. Summary and Report Guidelines Sheets for Exercises A & B	_____
9.	Read unit Summary	_____
10.	Exercises A and B completed with second subject	_____
11.	Report results with second subject—Summary and Report Guidelines Sheets for Exercises A & B	_____

DIRECTIONS AND RESPONSE SHEETS FOR EXERCISE A

In this exercise the subject will be faced with the task of learning what an "X Dimensional Representation" is. The name is irrelevant, but your subject won't know that. For your information an X Dimensional Representation is a figure with more than three sides and, therefore, more than three angles, and with one circle or ball within the figure. On your Total Figures Chart the positive examples of an X Dimensional Representation are 3A, 3B, 3D, 4A, 4B, and 4D. Note that possible irrelevant attributes are double right-side border and size of the figures.

Display the pictures one at a time in the order given below. Display them clearly and do not rush the subject. There is no time limit. At the point where the subject has correctly described the attributes of an X Dimensional Representation, test his conceptualization by having him tell you whether or not the displayed picture is an example *before* you tell him. A correct description of the concept should include *only* those attributes which are critical and *all* critical attributes. If a critical attribute is missing from the subject's description, then continue the exercise in the normal manner. If an irrelevant attribute is included, continue the exercise until he deletes it. The descriptive terms used by the subject need not be exactly like yours. For example consider "figures with 3 or more sides" to be the same as "triangles, squares, pentagons, and hexagons." "A double right-side border" is the same as "two lines on the right side." When he has correctly identified (by "yes" or "no") five figures in succession, stop the exercise.

Refrain from answering the subject's questions after the exercise has begun. They might try to manipulate you into helping them by asking, How should I describe that?; or I don't know what you are after, tell me more about the figure; or Am I on the right track? Answer these questions with a simple "I can't answer that question," or simply reread the directions which are pertinent to the question. Begin the exercise by reading the following directions:

> I am going to show you some pictures one at a time. Your task during this exercise is to determine what an "X Dimensional Representation" must look like. You, of course, should not know at this time what an X Dimensional Representation is. I will display a picture and tell you whether or not it is an example of that concept. Then I will ask you to tell me what the concept, "X Dimensional Representation," is. When you can correctly tell me what that concept consists of and correctly identify examples of it, the exercise is finished. I will inform you when your description of the concept is correct, then ask you to identify the

next five figures. I am going to help you a little by telling you that this picture is an example of an X Dimensional Representation. (Display picture No. 4B. The subject will not be able to see 4B or any other figures once you turn the page.)

Directions and Response Sheets for Exercise A—Continued

1. "Tell me—what do you think an X Dimensional Representation is?" (Paraphrase the subject's hypothesis here.)

Subject 1:_____

_____

Subject 2:_____

_____

2. Display picture No. 6B. Say to the subject, "This is not an example of an X Dimensional Representation. How would you describe an X Dimensional Representation now?"

Subject 1:_____

_____

Subject 2:_____

_____

3. Display picture 3E. "This is not an example. How would you describe an X Dimensional Representation now?"

Subject 1:_____

_____

Subject 2:_____

_____

4. Display picture 4A. "This is an example. How would you describe an X Dimensional Representation now?"

Subject 1:_____

_____

Subject 2:_____

_____

5. Display picture 3C. "This is not an example. What do you think an X Dimensional Representation is now?"

Subject 1: _____

Subject 2: _____

6. Display picture 2B. "This is not an example. What do you think an X Dimensional Representation is now?"

Subject 1: _____

Subject 2: _____

7. Display picture 1D. "This is not an example. What do you think . . .?"

Subject 1: _____

Subject 2: _____

8. Display picture 4D. "This is an example. What do you think . . .?"

Subject 1: _____

Subject 2: _____

9. Display picture 5B. "This is not an example. What do you think . . .?"

Subject 1: _____

Subject 2: _____

Display the remaining pictures in the following order: (Ask for a statement after each display. [+ = positive, − = negative example.])

10. 6E (−) Subject 1:_____, Subject 2:_____
11. 5E (−) _____
12. 1A (−) _____
13. 2D (−) _____
14. 3A (+) _____
15. 3D (+) _____
16. 2C (−) _____
17. 1C (−) _____
18. 5D (−) _____
19. 6A (−) _____
20. 4C (−) _____
21. 3B (+) _____
22. 2A (−) _____
23. 5C (−) _____
24. 4E (−) _____
25. 1E (−) _____
26. 1B (−) _____
27. 2E (−) _____
28. 5A (−) _____
29. 6C (−) _____
30. 6D (−) _____

Summary and Report Guidelines Sheets for Exercise A

1. Consider your subject's first hypothesis about the nature of an X
   Dimensional Representation after viewing picture 4B. Did the first
   subject's hypothesis include the components which are relevant?
   _____Yes _____No
   Did the second? _____Yes _____No
   What additional components or attributes were stated by subject 1?

   _____

   By subject 2?_____

   _____

2. Look at pictures 4B and 6B. The major difference between those two
   pictures is the number of circles or balls within the figure. Your subject
   had enough information at this point to revise his hypothesis to include
   "only one ball or circle within the figure." Did the first subject revise
   his statement in that manner? _____Yes _____No Did the
   second?_____Yes _____No Did he make any other changes?
   (1st) _____Yes _____No; (2nd) _____Yes _____No
   If yes, can you see why those changes were made? Explain: _____

   _____

3. Consider picture 3E. This figure might tend to confirm an inaccurate
   hypothesis, that is, that X Dimensional Representations are *squares*
   with one circle or ball within the figure. Did your first subject make
   this error? _____Yes _____No; second? _____Yes
   _____No If, in an earlier hypothesis, your subject thought that the
   double line or border on the right side of the figure was a critical
   attribute of an X Dimensional Representation, then picture 3E might
   tend to make the subject eliminate that part of his hypothesis. Did your
   first subject change his hypothesis in that manner? _____Yes
   _____No; (second?) _____Yes _____No Did either sub-
   ject change his hypothesis in regard to *both* the double border *and*
   the shape of the figure? _____Yes _____No

       Consider for a moment the task a child has when exposed to farm
   animals. If he is to learn the concept, "cow," he must build hypotheses
   about the attributes of a cow and add or delete according to exposures
   to cows. Equate the hypotheses of your subject with the thoughts of a
   child trying to conceptualize a "cow" and follow his progression to
   this point. For example, figure shape = cow size, double right-side
   border = horns, one circle = (You select another attribute) _____
   _____, two circles = _____.

Therefore, given picture 4B, the child might think a cow had to be so big, with a certain shape, have horns, and _____.

Given picture 6B his conceptualization would change such that _____

_____

If picture 3E was a lamb or some other farm animal other than a cow (differing in shape and size as well as not having horns), what might a cow be to the child after seeing picture 3E? _____

_____

4. After seeing picture 4A your subject's hypothesis could change to eliminate *squareness* and include "figures with angles and sides." Did your 1st subject change his hypothesis in that manner? _____Yes _____No; (2nd?) _____Yes _____No. He might have just added *pentagons* or five-sided figures to *squares* as the critical shapes to be considered. Did your subjects do this? (1st?) _____Yes _____No; (2nd?) _____Yes _____No. If your subject had previously eliminated the double right-side border, he might include it again at this point. Did he? (1st?) _____Yes _____No; (2nd?) _____Yes _____No. Relate your subject's hypothesis about X Dimensional Representations to the example of the child and his conceptualization of the cow.

_____

_____

5. The presentation of picture 3C as a negative example could give the subject no information to change his hypothesis if he attended to the absence of the double right-side border and simply used it to confirm his earlier hypothesis. Did your 1st subject do this? _____Yes _____No; (2nd?) _____Yes _____No. On the other hand, if your subject attended to the fact that the shape is different from any of those previously given, he might change his hypothesis to exclude triangles. Did your subjects do this? (1st?) _____Yes _____No; (2nd?) _____Yes _____No. Yet another condition is possible; your subject could have seen both changes from previous figures and be uncertain as to which change to make.

6. If picture 2B is used efficiently, and if previous pictures were used efficiently, then your subject could simply recognize that the concept,

X Dimensional Representation, must have a circle or ball within its borders. Did your 1st subject recognize this? _____Yes _____No; (2nd?) _____Yes _____No. Describe the conceptualization of the child with the "cow" at this point. _____

_____

7. Picture 1D really provides very little definite information if your subject's previous hypotheses included double right-side border, one circle and square, or pentagon shape. Picture 1D contains none of these attributes; so your subject would not know which one was critical and, therefore, be uncertain which could be eliminated or added. Did your subjects retain their earlier hypotheses after seeing 1D? (1st?) _____Yes _____No; (2nd?) _____Yes _____No.

8. Picture 4D should influence your subject's notions about the shape of X Dimensional Representations. Did it? (1st?) _____Yes _____No; (2nd?) _____Yes _____No. Relate the changes of your subject to the child's conceptualization of the "cow." _____

_____

_____

9. Pictures 5B, 6E, 5E, 6A, and 2D would not provide information for changes in your subject's hypothesis if he has been following the pattern described above. Did your subject make changes in his hypotheses? (1st?) _____Yes _____No; (2nd?) _____Yes _____No.

10. Picture 3A could be sufficient to land your subject on the correct hypothesis as to what the concept, X Dimensional Representation, is. At this point sufficient examples and information have been given to attain the concept. It is possible to eliminate the attribute, double right-side border, at this point. Did your 1st subject make this change? _____Yes _____No; (2nd?) _____Yes _____No.

11. Picture 3D could act to confirm a correct hypothesis about the shape and number of circles necessary for an X Dimensional Representation. Did your 1st subject identify the correct critical attributes at this point? _____Yes _____No; (2nd?) _____Yes _____No.

What is the state of the child's conceptualization of a "cow" at this point?_____

_____

12. Briefly describe the remainder of your subject's experiences with the exercise and the resulting changes in hypotheses (if any occurred).

_____

_____

_____

DIRECTIONS AND RESPONSE SHEET FOR EXERCISE B

In this exercise the subject will be faced with the task of learning what a Y Dimensional Representation is. Again, the name is irrelevant. For your information a Y Dimensional Representation is any figure with the double right-side border. Just as in Exercise A the subject will not know what a Y Dimensional Representation is. The positive examples of a Y Dimensional Representation are 2A, 2B, 2C, 2D, 2E, 4A, 4B, 4C, 4D, 4E, 6A, 6B, 6C, 6D, and 6E on the Total Figures Chart.

You will display the figures in the same way you did with Exercise A, however, you will not ask for a statement of hypothesis after each figure. The subject will keep his thoughts and hypotheses to himself until he is sure he knows what a Y Dimensional Representation is. At that point he will inform you that he knows what it is, and you can test him by having him identify (by "yes" or "no") the next five figures. His goal is to identify the concept as soon as possible. Begin the exercise by reading the following directions to your subject:

> I am going to show you some pictures one at a time. Your task is to identify the concept "Y Dimensional Representation." The only way I can help you is to show you a picture and tell you whether or not it is an example of a Y Dimensional Representation. *As soon as* you think you know what a Y Dimensional Representation is, simply say, "I know what it is," and I will let you try to identify the next five pictures before I tell you whether or not they are examples of the concept. You will not have to describe the concept at any time. If you make a mistake, we will go back to my identifying the pictures for you. You are allowed only one mistake. If you are incorrect the second time, the task is over and you lose. We will start with this picture which is an example of a Y Dimensional Representation. Please tell me each time you wish to see a new picture by saying, Go ahead.

1. Note how long the subject studies 4B.
2. The remaining pictures should be displayed in the following order:

(Draw a circle around the number of the picture last seen before the subject indicated that he knew the nature of the concept.)

2. 6B (+)	11. 5E (−)
3. 3E (−)	12. 1A (−)
4. 4A (+)	13. 2D (+)
5. 3C (−)	14. 3A (−)
6. 2B (+)	15. 3D (−)
7. 1D (−)	16. 2C (+)
8. 4D (+)	17. 1C (−)
9. 5B (−)	18. 5D (−)
10. 6E (+)	19. 6A (+)
20. 4C (+)	26. 1B (−)
21. 3B (−)	27. 2E (+)
22. 2A (+)	28. 5A (−)
23. 5C (−)	29. 6C (+)
24. 4E (+)	30. 6D (+)
25. 1E (−)	

31. If your subject correctly identified five pictures, ask him whether or not he viewed additional pictures to confirm his hypothesis *before* telling you, "I know what it is."

Summarize his answer here:

Subject 1:_____

_____

Subject 2:_____

_____

Summary and Report Guidelines Sheet for Exercise B

1. It is possible for your subject to identify the correct attributes of a Y Dimensional Representation with only eight figures or by the time he has seen 4D. At what number did your 1st subject indicate he knew what the concept was? _____; 2nd subject? _____. Did he make an error? (1st?) _____Yes _____No; (2nd?) _____Yes _____No. If yes, do you know the reason for the incorrect conceptualization?
Explain:_____

2. One of the major differences between Exercises A and B was the risk placed on the subject. In Exercise A there was practically no risk; the subject simply stated what he thought the concept was at that time. In Exercise B the subject was forced to decide when he was confident enough to take a chance that he knew what a Y Dimensional Representation was. Since the subject did not state his hypotheses to you, it is difficult for you to determine whether he "took a chance" as soon as he recognized the critical attributes or if he viewed extra figures to confirm his conceptualization. Question 31 will help you determine this. Did your subject "take a chance" as soon as he thought he knew what a Y Dimensional Representation was? Or did he confirm his hypothesis before saying, "I know what it is," by requesting to see extra figures?

Subject 1:_____

Subject 2: _____

3. Outline a real–life situation in which someone would learn a concept in the manner used in Exercise B. For example, an intelligence agent might hear of a certain project of a foreign power and be exposed to information which would help him to conceptualize the nature of the project. The urgency is there to identify the concept (project) as soon

as possible, but the need to be certain is also present.
Produce an example of your own below:

_____

_____

_____

_____

_____

_____

_____

_____

_____

_____

PICTURE SET FOR UNIT FOUR

(Note that the pictures are arranged and numbered according to the sequence in which they are to be used in Exercises A and B.)

Total Figures Chart

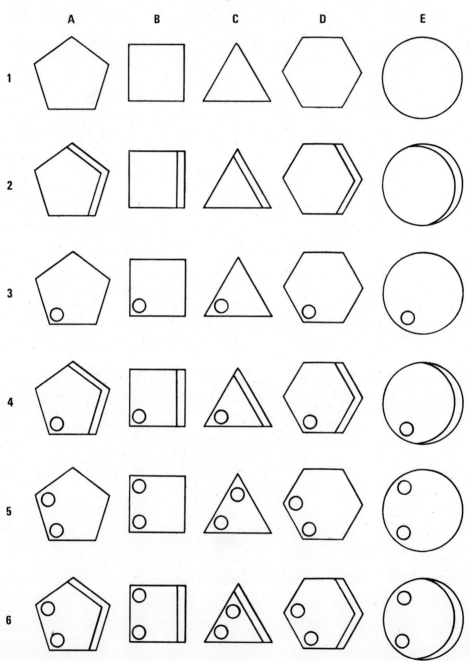

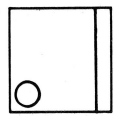

4B

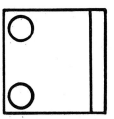

6B

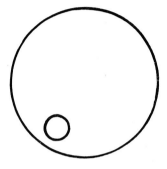

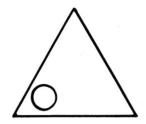

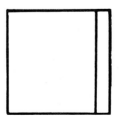

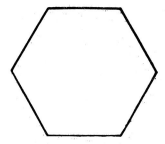

1D

4D

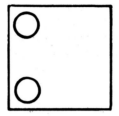

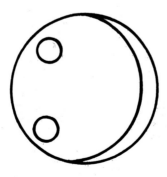

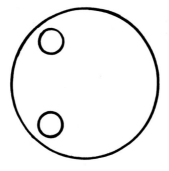

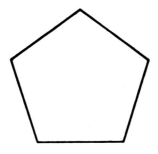

2D

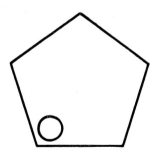

3A

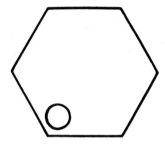

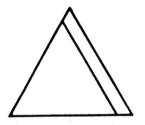

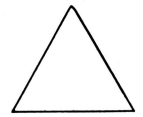

1C

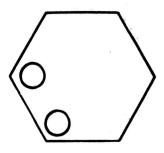

5D

149

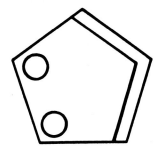

6A

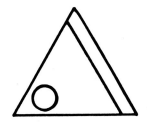

4C

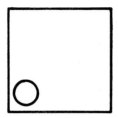

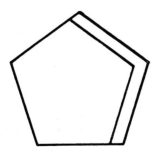

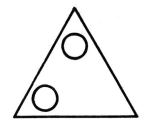

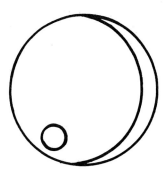

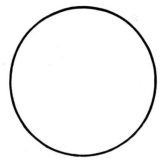

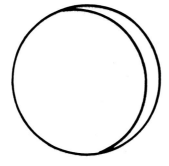

2E

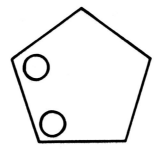

5A

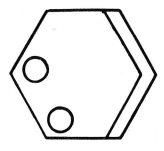

♦ SUMMARY

The Background material for this unit was designed to acquaint you with the means by which some psychologists investigate certain aspects of thinking. Thinking is, of course, a difficult item or activity for a scientist to explore, and the difficulties were explained briefly. A particular area within thinking, namely, the conceptual process, was defined and explained as it relates to learning and education.

The experience aspect of Unit Four was broken down into two exercises. In the first the subject shares his ideas about the concept to be learned with the person conducting the exercise. In the second exercise the subject does not share his hypotheses about the concept until he is sure he knows what the concept is. The material for the concepts consisted of geometric shapes with a varying number of circles within the figure and sometimes a double border. The student who completes both exercises and the accompanying materials will have a fair notion of how psychologists can research the area of cognition and how that research can provide information to be used in the classroom.

The question immediately comes up, How do you use notions about concept attainment in the classroom? It seems reasonable to assume that students learn a variety of new concepts in school. For example, in a math class there are "whole numbers," "rational numbers," "functions," "quadratic equations," and on and on. In the social studies class there is the concept of "democracy" or at a younger level the concepts of "town," "village," "county," "state," and "country" to be mastered. What happens to a child's concept of "poetry" when he is exposed to a variety of positive examples of poetry? Would you, as a teacher, want to arrange the positive examples so that certain attributes stand out and are recognized by the student? How would you use negative examples to help the student formulate the concept of "poetry"? Can you identify some instances in which it might be valuable for the student to verbally describe a concept so that you could recognize incorrect ideas? In Exercise A the subject constantly verbalized his ideas about the concept, X Dimensional Representation, and you could follow his progress. In Exercise B you could not follow your subject's progress in conceptualizing a Y Dimensional Representation. Which would be the most advantageous situation for you in the subject matter and age level you encounter (or will encounter)? Whether in a classroom or elsewhere, there are other considerations you should make in regard to concept learning.

What would happen if your subject "locked in" on the hypothesis he had after the first three exposures to figures? By "locked in," we mean that he simply held onto that hypothesis and ignored the further information available in subsequent exposures. You might say that he would simply not have a correct concept of what the thing was that you wanted him to know. You would probably be correct, but what are the implications of such a condition? Do you think that such a condition is possible? It would seem reasonable to assume that people who have stereotyped notions of various ethnic groups have "locked in" on certain attributes of the concept. For example, children often are exposed to the American Indian as a concept with buckskin clothes, primitive weapons, and a feathered head decoration. In spite of receiving information in the form of examples which should change the concept, the American Indian sometimes remains conceptualized as an old-west character. Can you think of some examples of this condition occurring with academic concepts?

A subject need not "lock in" on an hypothesis about a concept in order to have an incorrect notion about the nature of that concept. Consider the situation in Exercise B where a subject says, "I know what it is" and identifies the next five examples correctly. We might assume from this evidence that he has indeed correctly identified the attributes of the concept and tell him so. But what if he had an additional attribute as part of his conceptualization, and the five examples were accidentally arranged such that they would be negative in terms of that added attribute and negative in terms of the correct attributes? For instance, a student could hypothesize that a "sentence" must have a capital letter at the beginning, a period at the end, *and contain a prepositional phrase.* He would judge five sentences without verbs or subjects *and without prepositional phrases* to be negative examples of sentences. His judgment would be correct but for the wrong reason, i.e. he attended to an irrelevant attribute.

Still another problem which you might have encountered with the experience in this unit was that of memory. A subject could "forget" which examples previously seen were positive and which were negative. For example the subjects often "forget" whether or not the triangle was shown as a positive or negative example. It should certainly be kept in mind that memory could play a part in the rate at which conceptual processes progress.

How did other individual differences besides memory influence the efficiency and strategies employed by the subjects? Did your subjects approach the problem of attaining the concept in different ways? Would you expect that a pair of children exposed to several examples of a concept at the same time would attend to different attributes and arrive at a correct conceptualization at different times? It certainly seems possible and probable that a young child in Iowa watching television and seeing a new vehicle called a "Sea and Land Rover" would attend to different attributes of the machine from a child watching the same show in the Okeechobee Swamp of Florida. Whereas one might attend to its dry land capabilities, the other might be more likely to conceptualize the Rover as having wet terrain properties. Repeated exposures to examples of the concept might be necessary in order to arrive at near-equal concept attainment by the two children.

A variable influencing the efficiency of the conceptual processes and related to individual differences is the degree of abstraction/concreteness of the relevant or critical attributes. Those concepts with more abstract attributes are generally more difficult to learn or attain than those with more concrete attributes. For example the concept of "relativity" has attributes which are reasonably abstract, and therefore, the concept is not easily attained. On the other hand, the concept, earth, is fairly concrete and can be represented by photographs, drawings, and other representations which allow one to attain the concept quite easily. Did your subjects tend to seek out abstract attributes while doing Exercises A and B? Would you consider the critical attributes of X and Y Representational Dimensions to be abstract or concrete? If one of your subjects pursued the concepts by trying to analyze the name and associate the name with the figure, he was in a sense making the concept more abstract than it really was.

To what extent did the names, "X and Y Dimensional Representations," influence your subjects' strategies and efficiency at concept attainment? As can be the case with many concepts, the actual name associated with the concept will give no information about the nature of the concept. The name, in fact, can be spurious to the task of attaining the concept. This points up the mental or internal nature of concept attainment. It is very reasonable to assume that people have conceptualized many phenomena in their environment for which no particular word is available. In some cases when it is necessary to talk about the concept, we hear phrases like "that thingamajig" or "the whatsit." If the subject tries to use the word already established for the concept in order to learn the concept, then added difficulties can arise. The terms, X and Y Dimensional Representation, were arbitrarily chosen, and as a result do not aid in the attainment of the concept. Imagine a foreign agent during World War II trying to relate the term, "Mulberry Project," to the actual operation of building and moving huge concrete breakwaters across the English Channel. The point to be noted in this case is that the words associated with a concept might not aid in the attainment of the concept, and this fact should be taken into account by the teacher when concepts are to be learned.

Hopefully, the Background information, the Experience, and the Summary in this unit have stimulated some questions on your part about conceptual processes. It is not the author's intend to rehash and condense all the information psychologists have discovered about human conceptual processes. To the contrary, it was the purpose of this unit to generate questions about the topic and encourage the reader to pursue his curiosity into the Suggested Additional Activities and Readings. The information available for the reader who has some questions is considerable. For example there are answers to the questions: Why not show all the figures at once like in the Total Figures Chart? What changes occur in the subject's strategy, conceptualization, ease of conceptualization, and efficiency when all figures are shown at once? What are the different types of strategies used by subjects when the figures are shown in different sequences? What is the difference between a conjunctive and disconjunctive concept? The question that isn't always answered is, How is this information about conceptual processes relevant and applicable to my situation? That question the reader will probably have to answer for himself, and the answer could be, "It is not applicable. I can't use it." But whether the answer is yes or no, the reader must have the information before he can judge its usefulness. The Suggested Additional Activities which follow will add to your experience base, while the Suggested Additional Readings will provide further information about what other psychologists have done.

♦ SUGGESTED ADDITIONAL ACTIVITIES

1. Consider the differences in strategy by the subject and experimental procedures differences if you utilized the Total Figures Chart and allowed
the subject to see the complete universe of figures at one time. You could
arbitrarily pick some combination of attributes which are critical to a
concept. Identify to yourself the figures which are positive and those
which are negative. Inform your subject that he is to attain the concept
by pointing to the figure about which he wishes to have information.
Once he points to a figure, you can tell him whether or not it is a positive
example. The aspects of his behavior which are important to question are:
What hypothesis does he form? (You could ask him to state hypotheses
like in Exercise A.) What strategy does he use to select figures for identification? Does the presence of the Total Figures Chart increase the efficiency of the subject? An added wrinkle to this activity would be to
produce another Total Figures Chart which does not have the figures in
ordered horizontal and vertical sets. That is, you would randomly place
the figures on the page. Try to determine by testing subjects whether or
not the random order of the display influences the efficiency of the subject.

2. Use subjects at various age levels for Exercise A and B. Try to secure a
population which is similar, perhaps in regard to sex, achievement, socio–
economic class, school system, etc. Observe the differences in strategies
between the different age levels. You might also observe the differences
in the subjects' abilities to describe the concept. By recording the descriptions and splicing them together, you could assemble a fair cross section
of how a single attribute is described differently at different ages. You
might also watch for indications of children at certain ages attending to
particular attributes and not others. At a young enough age the differences
between the geometric shapes might be more noticeable than the double
right-side border. Or will they?

3. Many times we are exposed to positive and negative examples of a concept for only a very short period of time. It might occur while speeding
down a highway, or listening to a radio, or intermittently attending to a
lecturer. What is the effect of decreasing the exposure time for an example? Is it less critical to expose a negative example for a shorter period
of time than a positive example? By either limiting the amount of time a
subject can look at any figure or by limiting the exposure time of only the
negative examples you can begin to acquire information to answer ques-

tions like those above. Stress, usually in the form of time pressures, often tends to decrease performance with learning tasks. What aspect of performance will be decreased with the conceptual processes? Will the number of examples have to increase? Will the hypotheses be less well–formed? What is the effect of stress on risk as encountered in Exercise B?

♦ SUGGESTED ADDITIONAL READINGS

For Basic Information About Conceptual Processes

Bourne, L. E. Jr.; Ekstrand, B. R.; and Dominowski, R. L. *The Psychology of Thinking.* Englewood Cliffs, N.J.: Prentice-Hall, 1971, (esp. Part IV, Chapters 9, 10, 11 and 12).

Klausmeier, H. J. and Ripple, R. E. *Learning and Human Abilities.* New York: Harper and Row, 1971. (esp. Chapter 11, "Concepts and Principles").

For More Advanced Information

Bruner, J. S.; Goodnow, J. J.; and Austin, G. A. *A Study of Thinking.* New York: John Wiley and Sons, 1956.

Kintsch, W. *Learning, Memory and Conceptual Processes.* New York: John Wiley and Sons, 1970.

Klausmeier, H. J. and Harris, C. W. *Analyses of Concept Learning.* New York: Academic Press, 1966.

Piaget, J. *The Child's Conception of Number.* New York: W. W. Norton and Company, 1965.

Piaget, J. and Inhelder, B. *The Child's Conception of Space.* New York: W. W. Norton and Company, 1967.

For Information Regarding Specific Studies

Beane, W. E. and Lemke, E. A. "Group Variables Influencing the Transfer of Conceptual Behavior." *Journal of Educational Psychology* 62(1971):215–218.

Clark, C. D. "Monograph: Teaching Concepts in the Classroom: A Set of Teaching Prescriptions Derived from Experimental Research." *Journal of Educational Psychology* 62(1971):253–278.

Darnell, C. D. and Bourne, L. E. Jr. "Effects of Age, Verbal Ability, and Pretraining with Component Concepts on the Performance of Children in a Bidimensional Classification Task." *Journal of Educational Psychology* 61(1970):66–71.

Davis, J. K., and Klausmeier, H. J. "Cognitive Style and Concept Identification as a Function of Complexity and Training Procedures." *Journal of Educational Psychology* 61(1970):423–430.

Guthrie, J. T. and Baldwin, T. L. "Effects of Discrimination, Grammatical Rules, and Application of Rules on The Acquisition of Grammatical Concepts." *Journal of Educational Psychology* 61(1970):358–364.

Marx, D. J. "Intentional and Incidental Concept Formation as a Function of Conceptual Complexity, Intelligence, and Task Complexity." *Journal of Educational Psychology* 61(1970):297–403.

Nuthall, G. "An Experimental Comparison of Alternative Strategies for Teaching Concepts." *American Educational Research Journal* 5(1968):561–584.

UNIT 5

Learning

♦ BACKGROUND

The topics of previous units have included some of the individual variables which influence the learning process. In this unit the actual act of learning will be considered from the viewpoint of the psychologist. During the twentieth century learning has become a prominent area within the discipline of psychology, and the investigation of the learning process has become increasingly popular among research psychologists. The subjects used for investigation have ranged from one-celled animals through humans to computers, and the questions posed have had even a greater range. With this wealth of research data available about learning, it behooves anyone involved in the educational process to consider the ways it can be applied to everyday practice.

A single unit could not possibly cover all or even a major part of the theories, methods, principles, or procedures associated with learning, learning theory, learning research, or even applied human learning. The purpose of this unit will be to give the reader a minimal but sufficient amount of information in the area of learning in order to permit a meaningful experience with *one* of the multitude of ways psychologists study learning. The Suggested Additional Readings is the place to go for detailed facts, theory, and related information. The background and experience portion of this unit will provide only a concrete introduction to the topic of learning. The first point of information to be considered will be the definition of learning.

What does a psychologist mean when he talks about learning?

The definition of learning is a little like the definition of personality or intelligence in that it varies from one psychologist to another. For some psychologists it is an internal process which in one way or another changes the amount of knowledge, understanding, or just the mental state of the individual. A much more commonly accepted definition is that learning occurs when there is a change in the type, frequency, or sequence of a behavior. For example, a child is confronted with a sign that says "Stop," but to him it is just a meaningless figure to which he responds, "I don't know what that is." The initial behavior state, which we will call State 1, was the sequence of verbal behavior, "I don't know what that is." The later behavior state might be the verbalization of the word, "Stop." This later behavior state we will call State 2. An observer of the change from State 1 to State 2 might say that the child has learned to read. Strictly speaking, however, the child moved from one type of behavior to another in the presence of a single stimulus, or stimulus array. As that change in behavior occurred, learning took place. Learning research does more than just describe a change in behavior; it often attempts to clarify the theory behind the act of learning.

How do psychologists regard "learning theory"?

The study of "learning theory" concerns itself with how, why, and in what ways behavior changes. It should be noted at this point that there are many "theories" of learning which psychologists support. "Classical" learning theory, for instance, describes the change which occurs when a neutral stimulus (NS) becomes a conditioned stimulus (CS). Basically, the sequence of events in classical conditioning requires that an unconditioned stimulus (US) be identified first. A US is any stimulus which reliably elicits some particular response from a subject. That response is called an unconditioned response (UR). So, once you identify a US which consistently elicits a UR, you simply pair a neutral stimulus (NS) with the US, and it will shortly begin to elicit the UR. Once the NS elicits the UR, it is no longer neutral; so, it is called a conditioned stimulus (CS). The process of behavior change or learning is evident in the fact that the UR did not previously occur in the presence of the NS, but after the pairing of the NS and US, the UR will occur in the presence of the NS.

"Instrumental" learning involves the change which occurs when a response (R) is immediately followed by some form of reinforcement (SR) and the response (R) increases or decreases in frequency. For a more complete description of the use of instrumental learning principles applied to behavior change in applied settings the reader should consult Unit 7.

Both classical and instrumental learning are regarded as "conditioning" processes subsumed under the major category of learning. Conditioning implies that the learner need not consciously recognize or assist in the learning process; i.e., he is conditioned or programmed to respond by the action of external influences. Early theories of learning like the associationist theory are similar to conditioned learning. For example, the associationist would suggest that learning is simply the establishment of associations between stimuli (S) and responses (R). Such notions gave rise to the phrase "S-R psychology." It is reasonably easy to see how classical conditioning is a form of associationism.

On the other hand, there are theories of learning which are inferentially based and do not depend on a behavior change for demonstration of learning. Gestalt theories, for instance, deal with an individual's perception of himself and the world around him; therefore, learning is the process in which perceptions and the organization of perceptions change.

As stated many times previously, this book is built on the supposition that theory is not meaningful to a student until sufficient concrete knowledge has been gained through experience. With this in mind it is suggested that the reader pursue the Suggested Additional Readings for more information about the theories of learning after some experiences with learning as psychologists view it. It is not unusual for a psychologist to consider the variables influencing learning instead of theories of how or why learning takes place.

What variables influence learning?

If you completed Units One and Two already, you have encountered two variables, intelligence and personality, which can influence learning. Supposedly, differences in individual personalities can have an effect on the rate or amount learned by an individual, and it has long been believed that differences in intelligence account for some of the differences in learning observed in some students. The two aspects of individuality, personality and intelligence, are part of the larger category called individual differences. A sizable number of psychologists devote most of their research and study time to the topic of individual differences and the relationship it has to learning. On the other hand, the task to be learned is also an important variable to consider.

In Unit Nine you will be exposed to methods for analyzing a task or behavior chain, and it will become quite obvious that a seemingly simple task can be, in fact, highly complex and difficult to learn. So the psychologist has to consider the complexity of the task or behavior when discussing learning variables. When one considers "complexity," however, it is well to employ a wide definition so that such things as type of behavior, frequency of behavior, number of different responses in the chain, and the sequence of the behaviors in the chain are included. If an average ten-year-old student is learning to add 2 + 2, he is facing a vastly different task, in terms of complexity, from that of learning to solve linear trigonometric equations. The latter task requires different types of behaviors with different frequencies and with different sequences from the former. If he is solving such equations for a major architectural firm and earning a substantial salary, we must also recognize the motivational variable influencing learning.

The variable that most people would refer to as incentive, motivation, or reinforcement is subsumed under the general heading, environmental factors. This category includes all the external forces which have an effect on the learner. The teacher might be both an aversive stimulus (conditioned) and a dispenser of reinforcers. Since both of these forces or influences are external from the learner, they become part of the environmental influences.

To summarize, learning is thought to be influenced by three main factors; individual influences, task variables, and environmental influences. You will note that little mention has been made of "what" is learned, but, in fact, that is a major means of classifying learning research.

How can we classify what is learned?

There are a variety of different types of behavior which can be changed and, therefore, demonstrate that learning has occurred, but the classification of learned behaviors has been fairly consistently along the lines of: (1) physical skills or motor behaviors, (2) recognition or perceptual learning, (3) problem solving and (4) verbal skills.

The first category, physical skills or motor behavior learning, is often easy to see. The child learning to crawl and walk or the fledgling ballerina learning to pirouette are examples where rapid progress or changes in behavior are sometimes apparent even to the untrained eye.

The second category, perceptual learning, consists of the establishment of those behaviors which involve the sensory systems. The change from the state of not being able to recognize mother's voice to being able to discriminate it from others is an example of perceptual learning for an infant. For the older learner there are such skills as being able to distinguish one wine from another, or recognizing the difference between the smell of a baking pie as opposed to a burning pie. It is not difficult to generate examples from each of the sensory areas: vision, hearing, taste, touch, and smell. A human is not born with the perceptual skills we see exhibited each day; therefore, a logical assumption is that they must be learned.

The learning of problem solving strategies is much more subtle than other areas of learning such as motor skills. Imagine, for instance, that a child who is crawling across the kitchen floor becomes entangled and, from the child's viewpoint, entrapped within the four legs of a kitchen chair. The first attempt at solving this problem might be to whimper a bit, and thrust one's head backward and, perhaps, against the nearest leg or crossbar. If by some peculiar spatial arrangement the child is freed as a result of such behavior, then when faced with a similar problem in the future, we might see similar problem solving behaviors. And so in this manner, on up through the developmental stages, people can learn methods for solving problems. Some are more efficient than others. Some conform more closely to social mores than others. Some become formalized and are taught, while others are the result of fortuitious conditions. Regardless of the characteristics, they are all learned.

Verbal learning is considered by many psychologists to be a most important area of learning. Man has the capacity to communicate with his fellow man at a rather sophisticated level, and the learning of how to accomplish that communication begins early in infancy and continues well into adulthood. Verbal learning consists of all those changes in behavior which carry a person from the nonspeaking, nonverbal state to the position of speaking one or more of the recognized languages utilized on planet earth. The phonemic sounds, the sequences of sounds which form words, the meaning and meaningfulness of words, the sequence of words which form sentences, the variations in sequences of words which form sentences of different structure but not different meaning—all these are behaviors which must be learned and which come under the heading of verbal learning.

There are, of course, situations where more than one of the above mentioned areas of learning are combined into one task. For instance, learning to write seems to entail the learning of visual perceptual skills and motor skills. Figure skating with rhythm to music requires that the skater learn to hear the music and also move in certain patterns with the changes in the musical arrangement. Whereas the teacher often must work with the multiplicity of behaviors to be learned, the psychologist finds it necessary to isolate one aspect of learning by controlling the task and the environment presented to the subject. In the experience portion of this unit you will work with a particular type of isolated learning task called "paired associate learning."

What is meant by learning "paired associates"?

Psychologists, who research the problems of verbal learning, often use pairs of stimuli which the subject must learn to associate with each other. These "paired associates" are often pairs of words which would not otherwise be related, or they may be nonsense syllables, or in some cases geometric figures are used as the stimuli. In everyday life we learn many paired associates, for instance, the letter, "A," is paired with its associated name, "aye." The learning of a foreign language is often largely a practice of learning to pair well-known stimuli from one's native language with less well-known stimuli from a foreign language. In the experience part of this unit the subject will be confronted with learning to associate pairs of words.

♦ AN EXPERIENCE

How is the experience in this unit related to learning?

A particular theory within verbal learning literature will be emphasized in the experience part of this unit. It has been hypothesized that when a subject is given a set of paired associates to learn, the procedure he naturally must follow is to learn the individual members of the pairs before learning the associations between pairs. If this theory is true, then it would seem that a subject would learn more pairs accurately if he were exposed to one set of words first, then the other set, then the sets matched as pairs. For example, if Russian-English equivalents are to be learned, then it could be hypothesized that subjects will learn better if the list of Russian words is studied first, the list of English words studied second, and the Russian/English words matched as pairs presented last. An opposing procedure most commonly used would be to present the matched pairs only. The presentation of the individual words before the pairs is called a "two-stage" sequence; whereas the presentation of only the pairs is referred to as the "one-stage" sequence. You will note in the materials for the experience part of this unit that Russian/English paired associates are used. It is suggested that you use the two-stage procedure with one group and the one-stage procedure with another group, and compare the results.

The Experience Objectives and Suggested Procedure which follow will give you a much more detailed explanation of the experience.

Experience Objectives

1. You should arrange to have a number of subjects complete verbal learning sequences as described in "A Description of the Experience."
2. You should compare the test results utilizing the Data Summary Sheet.

Suggested Procedure for Achieving the Experience Objectives

1. Read "A Description of the Experience."
2. Conduct the experience the first time using yourself as the subject. Score your own test according to the directions.
3. Conduct the experience with subjects.
4. Complete the Data Summary Sheet.

Progress Chart

Activity	Check each space when completed
1. Read "A Description of the Experience"	_____
2. Conduct experience using yourself as subject	_____
3. Conduct experience with Group 1 subjects	_____
4. Conduct experience with Group 2 subjects	_____
5. Complete the Data Summary Sheet	_____

A Description of the Experience

Introduction: As stated in the Background information, the type of learning to be used in this experience will be verbal learning with emphasis on the learning of paired associates. More specifically, the pairs will be made up of twenty Russian and twenty English words. The task of the learner will be to write as many of the pairs as possible after six minutes of exposure to the materials. Simply having a group of students memorize some Russian and English words is not much of an experience; so you will have two groups: one group will have six continuous minutes to look at and learn the pairs on Stimulus Sheet No. 3, while another group will look at the list of English words on Stimulus Sheet No. 1 for two minutes; then the list of Russian words on Stimulus Sheet No. 2 for two minutes; and finally, the list of Russian/English pairs on Stimulus Sheet No. 3 for two minutes. Note that each group gets to work for a total of six minutes, but the second group is exposed to one half of each pair, then the other half of each pair, then the complete list of paired words. At the end of the six minutes both groups will be given two minutes to write as many of the pairs as possible on a blank sheet of paper. During this final testing period, the subjects should not be able to see any of the Stimulus Sheets.

The experience should be conducted with one subject at a time. There is not a designated number of subjects which you should work with; but keep in mind that when a psychologist performs research with a topic like this, he will utilize large numbers of subjects in each group—usually a minimum of thirty persons per group. Subjects who can speak or comprehend a Slavic language should not be used for the experience.

Select a quiet location for the experience and have the three stimulus sheets, a pencil, a blank sheet of paper, and a stopwatch ready.

Directions: For one group read the following directions:

Your task is to learn as many pairs of Russian and English words on this list as possible in the time I give you. (Do not show the list at this time.) The procedure we will follow will be to have you look at a list of English words and memorize as many as you can in two minutes; then you will have two minutes to look at a list of Russian words; then you will have two minutes to work with a list of Russian and English pairs from the other two lists. At the very end I will ask you to write on this blank sheet of paper as many correctly matched pairs of Russian and English words as you can remember. Are there any questions? (Try not to give off-hand information in answer to questions. Simply reread the appropriate directions.)

Hand Stimulus Sheet No. 1 to the subject and say:

"You have two minutes to learn the words on this sheet—begin." *At the end of two minutes take back Stimulus Sheet No. 1 and hand Stimulus Sheet No. 2 to the subject while saying:* "You have two minutes to learn the words on this sheet—begin."

At the end of two minutes take back Stimulus Sheet No. 2 and hand Stimulus Sheet No. 3 to the subject while saying: "You have two minutes to learn the pairs of words on this sheet—begin."

At the end of two minutes take back Stimulus Sheet No. 3 and hand a blank sheet of paper to the subject while saying: "Write as many of the pairs of words as you can on this sheet. You will have two minutes. Remember the pairs must be correctly matched to count."

For the other group read the following directions:

Your task is to learn as many pairs of Russian and English words on this list as possible in the time I give you. (Do not show the list at this time.) You will have six minutes to study the Russian and English pairs. At the end of six minutes I will ask you to write on this blank sheet of paper as many correctly matched pairs of Russian and English words as you can remember. Are there any questions?

Hand Stimulus Sheet No. 3 to the subject and say: "You have six minutes to learn the pairs of words on this sheet—begin."

At the end of six minutes take back Stimulus Sheet No. 3 and hand a blank sheet of paper to the subject while saying: "Write as many of the pairs of words as you can on this sheet. You will have two minutes. Remember the pairs must be correctly matched to count."

Scoring: You will note that Russian letters are not identical to English letters, for instance, the "T"-like letter always appears in upper case, and "H" and "a" are the same size as the "T." When you score the pairs, first count the number of correctly matched pairs without eliminating any for incorrect production of letters or minor misspelling. Obtain a second score by counting the number of correctly matched pairs with the condition of eliminating those where the letters are incorrectly produced or the word is misspelled. On the Data Summary Sheet the first count will be "Score A," and the second count will be "Score B."

Data Summary Sheet

Use this sheet to summarize the information from each group after you have completed the experience with all subjects.

How many subjects did you use for Group 1? _____

How many subjects did you use for Group 2? _____

If you added all the Group 1, Score A's together, what was the total? _____

What was the mean* for Group 1, Score A? _____

If you added all the Group 2, Score A's together, what was the total? _____

What was the mean for Group 2, Score A? _____

If you added all the Group 1, Score B's together, what was the total? _____

What was the mean for Group 1, Score B? _____

If you added all the Group 2, Score B's together, what was the total? _____

What was the mean for Group 2, Score B? _____

---

* The mean is computed by dividing the sum or total score for the group by the number of subjects in that group. For example, if the scores of thirty subjects in Group 1 equalled 90, then the mean would be $90 \div 30 = 3.0$.

Stimulus Sheet No. 1

смотр
отара
век
енот
навет
рвота
аттестат
север
округ
камень
ахать
касатка
вертеть
ровно
хна
уместно
тоска
уехать
хватать
носка

Stimulus Sheet No. 2

review
flock
century
raccoon
slander
vomiting
certificate
north
region
stone
exclaim
swallow
twirl
equal
henna
appropriately
melancholy
leave
suffice
carrying

Stimulus Sheet No. 3

смотр	review
отара	flock
век	century
енот	raccoon
навет	slander
рвота	vomiting
аттестат	certificate
север	north
округ	region
камень	stone
ахать	exclaim
касатка	swallow
вертеть	twirl
ровно	equal
хна	henna
уместно	appropriately
тоска	melancholy
уехать	leave
хватать	suffice
носка	carrying

♦ SUMMARY

A topic as extensive as learning cannot be covered in any detail in a single chapter nor in the Background portion of a single unit. The Background part of this unit, therefore, was meant to be simply a brief introduction to several aspects of learning as it relates to the psychology of the educational process. The definitions used by psychologists, the variables influencing learning, the types of learning, learning theory, verbal learning, and paired associate learning were discussed briefly in order to minimally prepare the reader for the experience.

The experience was designed as a two-group study of the two-stage theory of paired associate learning. Subjects were to be divided into two groups; one group which saw the individual members of the pairs before seeing the pairs, and another group which saw the pairs only. The two groups were to be compared on the basis of two scores; one score overlooked the misspelling of the Russian words which were to be paired with their English equivalents, the other score took into account the misspellings and the incorrectly produced Russian letters. The two stage theory of verbal or paired associate learning suggests that people naturally learn the members of the pairs before learning the pairings. It was expected, therefore, that the group seeing the individual members before seeing the pairs would score higher on the test.

Which group had the highest mean score for those subjects you tested? If you found that the group seeing the pairs in two stages had the greater mean, then the experience went as expected, and we can consider the extent to which this data supports the two-stage theory. Of course, it would be unwise to suggest that the theory is "proven" as a result of such limited results, but now you have a certain amount of firsthand evidence in favor of the notion that people learn the members of the pairs before learning the pairings. On the other hand, if the group which only saw the pairs for six minutes achieved the greater mean, then you have evidence which suggests that you should begin to suspect the application of the theory in the manner employed in the experience. In either case it would not be prudent to believe that the results of the experience are the last word regarding the validity of the theory.

Your scores for the two groups were probably different, that is, one score was probably greater than the other. Is it sufficient for them just to be different in order for a psychologist to say that there is, indeed, a reliable difference between the groups? That question can be phrased another way, How different do the scores have to be in order for the researcher to be confident that the differences are not the result of chance? The answer to such a question lies in the statistical procedure used by psychologists to evaluate data. By converting apparent differences into statistical differences, the researcher can determine the probability that the difference in scores was due to chance. If a psychologist reports that the difference between groups was significant at the .01 level, he is saying that he used a statistical procedure to determine that the difference could occur by chance only once in a hundred times. Odds of one in one hundred are certainly attractive gambling odds and are considered as fairly acceptable by researchers in most cases. The statistical tools used by psychologists have a variety of names; mean, mode, median, standard deviation, variance, t-test, analysis of variance, correlations, and many more. There are several good statistics books to which one can refer when questions arise regarding the treatment of data. In fact, there are a number of books especially prepared for the educator who wishes to understand statistical manipulations without the extensive knowledge necessary for application. Keep in mind that without proper experimental controls or statistical application, apparent differences, such as you might have observed in your experience, are not always regarded by psychologists as reliable.

Again considering the results of your experience; assuming that the results are reliable, what are the possible implications of what you found? How would you use the information derived from this experience in an educational setting? Can you identify situations which involve the learning or teaching of items like the Russian/English pairs? If the two-stage approach appears to be most advantageous to the learner, then what can the teacher do to provide such an approach? Consider the problem of teaching the letters of the English alphabet to a child and also teaching the names of the letters. Would it seem to be reasonable to work first on recognizing the letters and the individual names before learning the associations? To what extent do you think studies like the experience are useful for practical application?

While conducting the experience, you had an opportunity to observe a variety of factors which could influence the learning of the pairs. Did you note individual differences between subjects in terms of personality, intelligence, and memory? For instance, what effect did anxiety play in the effective learning of the pairs in the situation which you observed? To what extent might an extroverted individual perform better at this task than an introverted individual? Did any of your subjects claim to have a poor memory for such tasks as you presented? Could memory abilities differ from individual to individual and, therefore, result in learning differences between individuals even within one group? Anxiety, introversion, extroversion, and memory are aspects of the individual differences which were discussed in the Background section of this unit as a possible variable influencing learning.

Another variable which can influence learning is the conditions existing in environment. This was the variable which was controlled or manipulated in the experience. Although the final task was the same for both groups, the materials used and the instructions followed in order to prepare for that final task were different; therefore, the environment for one group was different from that of the other group. The question asked of the data derived from the experience was whether or not the difference in the environmental conditions during the practice would influence learning.

Along with the obvious differences in group treatment there were probably also differences in the degree to which individuals were reinforced for participating as subjects. Did you notice that some subjects were more enthusiastic about the experience or seemed to enjoy it more than others? Is it possible that those people were more rewarded for working with you? What influence might that reward have on learning? How could you take advantage of reinforcement in classroom learning? Could you make a learning task rewarding even if it were not naturally so? To what extent could differences in the natural reward value in learning a task account for the differences in learning abilities and achievement in a classroom?

Along with the fluctuation in the degree of reinforcement from subject to subject, there were several other extraneous variables which verbal learning researchers would have to take into account. First, there is the problem of the Russian letters being different from English letters. If the subjects had never seen Russian letters before, they would have to learn to recognize how they differed from English letters and also how to reproduce them for the final test. But they were instructed to learn the pairs—do you have evidence that learning the letter shapes was ignored? Or did your subjects manage to learn some of the pairs and the letters at the same time? Unfortunately it is difficult to determine from this experience how much of the difficulty of learning the pairs is attributable to the pairs themselves and how much can be attributed to a problem like the letter variation.

The syllable structure of the Russian words was also somewhat different from that of English words and could have become an additional item to be learned during the practice period. Syllable structure, like letter structure, might be difficult to learn because of the previously learned English letter and syllable structure. Did you see evidence of English structure being used in place of Russian structure? Some psychologists have theorized that prior learning can interfere with or inhibit later learning. That is, a subject will have difficulty learning new material because of the interference of old material which is similar. To what extent would prior learning in school tend to inhibit later school learning? Can you cite specific instances? What about the situation in which a child learned something at home which had to be replaced by something else at school—the word, "ain't," for instance? Can you identify educational situations where ostensibly only two items need be learned and paired, but where, in fact, several items like letter shape must also be learned? Knowing precisely what is to be learned often saves the teacher and student considerable frustration.

There are other variables like letter shape which are evident in the word pairs given. Researchers have found the meaningfulness or "shock value" of words can influence the degree to which the words will be remembered by subjects. "Vomiting," for example, is a word which might tend to arouse more anxiety in subjects than a word like "review," and as a result, "vomiting" could be remembered longer. Did you find that to be true? Did you see certain words repeatedly on the tests? Why do you suppose that occurs? Could certain words be more meaningful to some subjects than they are to others? How is that related to the applied educational situation? Is it possible that some things students learn are more meaningful than others? What would be the effect of such a situation? What could you do to take advantage of such a situation as a teacher, as a student?

As you went through the experience, you were a student, and, hopefully, you learned something about the way man learns. Learning is undoubtedly one of the most remarkable characteristics of the human species, and for that reason it has been the focus for innumerable theories, hypotheses, superstitions, etc. It is up to the student to sort through the volumes of words and ideas to come to independent decisions about the most reasonable and workable concepts of learning. The study of human learning can be a lifelong endeavor for those who wish to pursue it. At this point you have a start and the Suggested Additional Activities and Readings will speed you on your way.

♦ SUGGESTED ADDITIONAL ACTIVITIES

1. There are other ways of evaluating the differences in strategies for presenting material to be learned. Rather than use the *one trial* design as in the experience for this unit, you might want to have the subject repeat the trials until performance reaches a criterion level. This simply means that you would arbitrarily select a number of pairs, say ten, which the subject would be required to learn correctly. Just as in the earlier experience the pairs would be presented in six minute blocks, either in the one-stage or two-stage sequence; and the test would again be given after the six minutes, but this time the subject continues to repeat trials until he gets ten (or whatever other number you select) correct. A convenient method for illustrating the performance of your subjects is to plot on a graph the number correct on each test for each trial. You would want to use a graph like the one below:

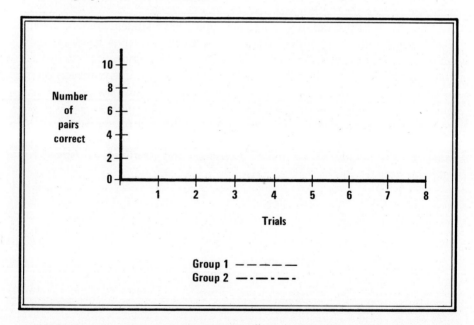

If the presentation sequence of the stimuli (the pairs) does make a difference in learning, then you would expect that the curve on the graph for one group would have a steeper slope or climb more rapidly and reach the criterion level (ten) in less trials than the curve of the other group.

2. Would young children react differently to this task from the way adults do? What evidence do you have to support your conclusion? It might be an interesting project to investigate the differences in learning which

occur developmentally, that is, at different age levels. It will probably be necessary for you to make a new set of paired associates because the Russian/English word pairs will probably be too difficult for very young children. Pairings could be made from shapes and colors such as a rectangle with a blue spot, a square with a red spot, etc., or shapes and figures like a square with a stick-figure man, a triangle with a stick-figure horse, etc. Essentially the same time limits can be used for both the one-stage and the two-stage sequence. Either the procedure used in the experience or the one described in Suggested Activity No. 1 could be used with most age groups. You might discover, however, that the criterion set by you for older students will not be attainable by younger students —or will it?

♦ SUGGESTED ADDITIONAL READINGS

For Basic Information About Learning

Borger, R., and Seaborne, A. E. M. *The Psychology of Learning*. Baltimore: Pelican Books, 1966.

Johnson, O. E. *Psychology of School Learning*. New York: Wiley & Sons, 1971.

Jones, J. C. *Learning*. New York: Harcourt, Brace & World, 1967.

Logan, F. A. *Fundamentals of Learning and Motivation*. Dubuque: William C. Brown Company Publishers, 1969.

Mednick, S. A. *Learning*. Englewood Cliffs: Prentice-Hall, 1964.

Walker, E. L. *Conditioning and Instrumental Learning*. Belmont, California: Brooks Cole, 1967.

For Advanced Information About Learning

Garry, R., and Kingsley, H. L. *The Nature and Conditions of Learning*. Englewood Cliffs: Prentice-Hall, 1970.

Hall, J. F. *The Psychology of Learning*. Philadelphia: Lippincott, 1966.

Hall, J. F. *Verbal Learning and Retention*. Philadelphia: Lippincott, 1971.

Hilgard, E. R. *Theories of Learning*. New York: Appleton-Century-Crofts, 1956.

Kintsch, W. *Learning, Memory and Conceptual Processes*. New York: Wiley and Sons, 1970.

McLaughlin, B. *Learning and Social Behavior*. New York: The Free Press, 1971.

For Specific Information About Particular Aspects of Learnings

Grose, R. F., and Birney, R. C. *Transfer of Learning*. New York: Van Nostrand, 1963.

Hall, J. F. *Readings in the Psychology of Learning*. Philadelphia: Lippincott, 1967.

Johnson, P. E. *Learning: Theory and Practice*. New York: Crowell, 1971.

Sluckin, W. *Imprinting and Early Learning*. Chicago: Aldine, 1965.

UNIT 6

Teacher-Student Interaction

♦ BACKGROUND

Previous units looked at individual differences in the student. In this unit we will begin to consider the teacher as part of the total process of classroom learning. A number of educational psychologists believe that the behavior exchange from teacher to student or from student to teacher is a more important consideration than one individual's characteristics, skills, or potential. The general proposition in this case is that a teacher who skillfully controls classroom interaction can overcome the problems of a child who is, perhaps, anxious, impermeable, or of low intelligence. One tool which is used to measure and evaluate classroom behavior is called *interaction analysis*. In this unit you will learn how to observe and collect interaction analysis data from the classroom. Before going into detail about the actual experience in this unit, let's look at some basic information about interaction analysis.

What is meant by classroom interaction?

A teacher and several students in a classroom can interact in a number of ways. For example, if two students are pushing and hitting each other, they are interacting in a physical manner. A silent type of interaction can occur between teacher and student when a stern or reproachful look is given. But the type of interaction at which we will look is verbal, i.e., what happens when people talk to each other.

How does one go about observing verbal interaction in a classroom?

Human beings seem to "see" more and remember more about what has happened if they have some specific things to look for while observing. When

193

a group of people are given the same things to look for, there is generally more agreement or reliability in their observation reports. Therefore, inter-action analysis requires that observers look for certain categories of verbal behavior which can occur in a classroom.

What categories are used to analyze classroom behavior?

The method of interaction analysis employed is a modification of that described by Ned Flanders.* Following is the list of categories which will be used:

1. Joking, praise or supportive statements: Supportive statements are defined as those in which the teacher simply restates or paraphrases a student comment.
2. Teacher questions to the class: Whenever a teacher or the person who is assuming the usual teacher role asks a question *which should elicit a response from a student,* it is categorized as a No. 2 behavior.
3. Teacher lecture: This is a broad category. It includes almost all statements from the teacher to the class which are subject matter oriented. When a teacher answers a student question about the topic at hand, he is lecturing —even though it might take only a few seconds. The explanation of a problem or task is usually lecture.
4. Teacher directions to the class or to an individual: This category includes all the statements a teacher makes when he tells students what to do— even those of a disciplinary nature. This category occurs most often when an assignment or task has been given to the class.
5. Student statements to the teacher or to the class: Answers to questions and student reports fall into this category. Generally, this category can be considered as any student verbal behavior which is not a question.
6. Student questions to the teacher or to the class: This category includes queries from a student which are or should be answered by the teacher or another student.
7. Silence or confusion.

How do you record data for analyzing student-teacher interaction?

At three second intervals you will assign one of the seven categories to the verbal behavior occurring during the previous three–second interval. You record this in a vertical column using the number of the category. Thirty seconds of lecture would look like this:

* N. Flanders, "Teacher Influence, Pupil Attitudes, and Achievement" (Washington, D.C.: U.S. Dept. HEW, 1965).

3
3
3
3
3
3
3
3
3
3

When you begin observing, you shouldn't be too concerned with the accuracy of three second spacing. Check the number of tallies you have after a minute interval and begin to get some idea whether you are too slow or too fast. After some practice you will operate at a fixed and reasonably accurate rate.

What do you do with the "raw data" recorded in columns?

After all the data has been gathered, the tallies must be transferred to a 7 x 7 matrix like Figure 6.1.

There is a tally (1) in the 2–3 cell. Place another (1) in the 4–6 cell. The first number of any pair is the *row* number, the second number of any pair is the *column* number. Therefore, each cell in the matrix has a name which is made up of two numbers, the row number and the column number.

What is the procedure for transferring tallies to the matrix?

Suppose after observing a class, you have a series of tallies like this:

3	1	6
2	1	6
3	1	6
3	3	3
3	3	3
4	3	3
6	3	4
4	3	5
4	3	5
3	4	6
1	5	6
	5	3
	5	

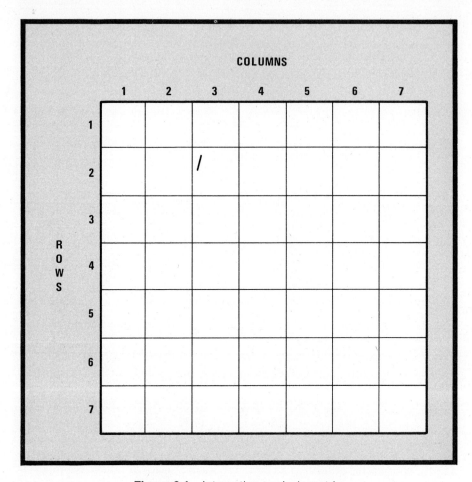

Figure 6.1 Interaction analysis matrix.

In order to place these tallies on the matrix you must take *overlapping, consecutive* pairs. The first pair is 3–2; so you would place a tally (1) in the 3–2 cell of the matrix.

The second pair is 2–3; so you would place a tally in the 2–3 cell. The third pair is: (check one)

_____A. 3–3

_____B. 3–4

so you would place a tally (1) in the 3–3 cell. You would continue to place tallies on the matrix until all overlapping, consecutive pairs in your data

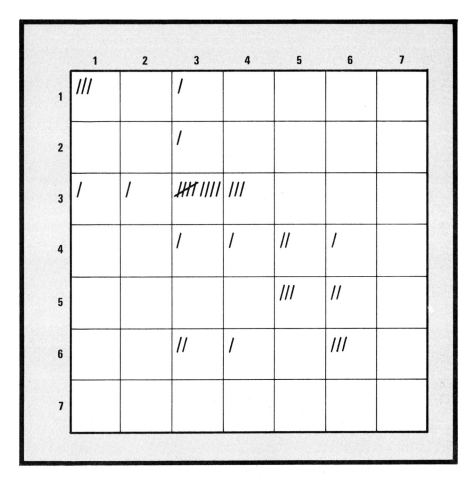

Figure 6.2 Interaction analysis matrix with tallies.

have been transferred to the matrix. For the above tallies the matrix would look like Figure 6.2.

What information can you get from the matrix?

The long columns of numbers in the raw data are hard to analyze in any meaningful way. But, there are several pieces of information about the interaction which can be readily seen from the matrix. The ones you will be concerned with in this experience are:

Primary patterns
Secondary patterns
High frequency categories
Low frequency categories

How do you locate primary patterns?

1. Primary patterns are based on the probabilities that certain behaviors will (and did) occur. You start by locating the cell with the greatest number of tallies in it. This is the behavior which had the greatest probability for that class period. For the completed matrix above the most probable behavior sequence was 3–3. (There are 9 tallies in the 3–3 cell.) We can say that if you entered the class at any time during the recorded period, the most probable behavior occurring would be teacher lecture (3) followed by teacher lecture (3).

2. Now, we want to find what behavior was most probable after a 3 *if another 3 did not occur.* Another way of saying this is: If we want to move from 3–3, then 3–? is probable? Cell 3–4 has 3 tallies which is more than the 3–1 or the 3–2 cells. Therefore interaction primarily moved from 3–3 ⟶ 3–4 ⟶? Remember that the first number of a cell's name is always the row and the second number is the column.

3. We now have a 4 behavior (teacher directions) occurring. What most often followed a 4? (or 4–? cell has the greatest number of tallies?)
   4–5 cell has 2 tallies;
   4–3, 4–4, 4–6 all have 1 tally;
   so a 4 behavior was most often followed by a 5. The pattern is now:
   3–3 ⟶ 3–4 ⟶ 4–5 ⟶ 5–?

4. Follow out the rest of the pattern using the technique as described above. You should develop a 3–3 ⟶ 3–4 ⟶ 4–5 ⟶ 5–5 ⟶ 5–6 ⟶ 6–6 ⟶ 6–3. You will note that by drawing lines on the matrix from each cell in the pattern to the next, the pattern closes: i.e., it is circular; you come back to the cell where you began. This is generally true of a primary pattern.

5. As we stated earlier, primary patterns are based on the probability that some particular behaviors would (and did) occur. Therefore, the primary pattern tells you what sequence of behaviors was most likely to occur in that classroom. For example, if you knew that the primary pattern for a classroom was 3–3 ⟶ 3–2 ⟶ 2–5 ⟶ 5–3, then anytime you entered that class and found the teacher lecturing, you could predict that

the next behavior to occur would be a "teacher question" followed by a "student statement" followed by more teacher lecture.

How do you locate secondary patterns?

1. Use the same technique as you used for primary patterns but begin the pattern with some behavior sequence which was *not* the most probable but second or third highest. In the matrix above, you might start with the 1–1 cell. You will find that most secondary patterns will lead into the primary pattern.

2. In the case of two cells having an equal number of tallies (i.e., they are equally probable), you may choose to follow only one or follow both and develop two branches off one initial pattern.

3. Secondary patterns tell you what sequences of behavior are likely to occur outside the primary pattern. They also tell you how the interaction comes back to the primary pattern.

What are high and low frequency categories?

It is useful for an observer to know which category of behavior occurred most or least often. For example, if a teacher did not mean to lecture to the students during a class, it would be useful to know from an observer's data just how much lecture did occur. In order to locate this information, percentages must be calculated. The question being asked is simply: Behavior Category X is what percent of the total interaction? To compute this, add all the tallies so you know how many you have in total on the matrix. Next, add all the tallies in a particular *column*. Divide the total number of tallies in the column by the sum total on the matrix, and you have the percent for that column. Of course, the column represents a behavior category; so you also have the percent of the total which that category took up during the observation. For example, in the matrix above the total number of tallies is 35. Suppose we want to know how much of the total interaction was taken up by teacher lecture, Category 3. We add the number of tallies in column three, which comes to 14. Fourteen divided by 35 equals .40, or 40 percent. Teacher lecture accounted for 40 percent of the total interaction in that classroom. There is no other behavior which accounted for a higher percentage of the total classroom interaction; so for that class we would say that Category 3, teacher lecture, was the *high frequency category*. The total number of tallies for Category 7 was zero, so that was the *low frequency category*.

♦ AN EXPERIENCE

What is the purpose of the experience in this unit, and how does it relate to interaction analysis?

Obviously, there are a great many verbal behaviors occurring in the average classroom, and the outcomes of those behaviors are different according to the approach one takes when observing. The experience in this unit is designed to allow you to observe and record certain verbal behaviors just as a psychologist might who uses the interaction analysis technique. In addition, you should evaluate the outcome of the interaction in much the same way a psychologist would who is testing a hunch or hypothesis about what happens in classrooms. Hunches are usually based on casual observations and subjective analysis, so therefore, they are not always reliable or accurate. In order to convert a hunch into positive information, a psychologist will state the hunch in the form of an hypothesis, and afterwards, collect data which should either support or weaken the hypothesis. In this unit experience, you should use interaction analysis data to evaluate several hypotheses about teacher-student interaction. The Experience Objectives below give you a more detailed description of what you should do.

Experience Objectives

1. You should record teacher-student interaction in three recitation or discussion-type classes.
2. You should prepare an interaction analysis matrix for each class.
3. You should write a report for each class.

Suggested Procedure for Achieving the Experience Objectives

1. Read over the Classroom Interaction Analysis Experience Description Sheet.
2. Secure permission and observe a classroom.
3. Transfer the data to a matrix.
4. Read the Sample Interaction Analysis Report and write a rough draft of your report.
5. Use the checklist on the Experience Description Sheet to revise your report.
6. Follow steps 2, 3, 4, and 5 to complete classroom observations 2 and 3.

Progress Chart

	Activity	Check each space when completed.
1.	Read Experience Description Sheet	_____
2.	First classroom observation	_____
3.	Matrix completion, first observation	_____
4.	First classroom observation report complete	_____
5.	Second classroom observation	_____
6.	Second classroom observation matrix	_____
7.	Second classroom observation report	_____
8.	Third classroom observation	_____
9.	Third classroom observation matrix	_____
10.	Third classroom observation report	_____

Classroom Interaction Analysis Experience Description Sheet

1. You are to observe and record data from three (3) classes. Classes are to be of a recitation nature—as opposed to lecture–type sessions. If a class is listed in the class schedule or catalog as being a recitation, or if the teacher calls it a recitation, that is sufficient. You might discover from your data collection that it does not fit your definition of a recitation class. Each class you observe should be at least thirty minutes long. You may observe at any level you wish, i.e., college, high school, elementary. You may observe in any discipline you wish, i.e., math, psychology, education, etc.

2. You are to write a report for each observation. The report should include an interaction analysis matrix.

3. Be sure to request permission to observe before collecting data in *any* classroom.

4. In your report you are to mention one of the following hypotheses and state whether or not your data supports it.

    a. Silence following a teacher question is an aversive stimulus which the teacher will avoid by answering his own question. The "hunch" here is that each time the teacher asks a question, the class will not respond, therefore, you would record silence. An aversive stimulus is something that is noxious or disagreeable. Silence in a classroom could be an aversive stimulus if answers are desired. If the silence is aversive enough, the teacher might form the habit of ending the silence by lecturing. This particular hypothesis would be supported if you found a primary or secondary pattern of 3–3 ⟶ 3–2 ⟶ 2–7 ⟶ 7–3. Oddly enough, the students might also learn that the aversive stimulus (silence) would end if they *don't* volunteer answers but wait for the teacher to lecture.

b. Reinforcement of student responses (either in the form of questions or statements) by teacher praise or support (Category No. 1) will yield a high frequency of student responses. The opposite would also be true. This statement describes the basic operation in positive reinforcement. If the teacher praises or supports (Category 1) student statements (Category 5), those students are more likely to make statements. Support for this hypothesis would be a primary or secondary pattern in which Category 1 followed Category 5.

c. Student questions are discriminative stimuli for teacher lecture. Discriminative stimuli (S^D) are those signals in the presence of which a response frequently occurs. For example, a red light is an S^D for the driver's "stopping" behavior. In the case of this hypothesis it is suggested that a student question will be a signal for the teacher to begin lecturing. Support for this hypothesis would be a high frequency of the pattern, 6–3 ⟶ 3–3. The teacher, of course, has many other options like restating the question (Category 1) or turning the question back to the class (Category 2).

5. Here is a partial checklist for writing a report.

a. Is it written in third person? "The experimenter" rather than "I."
b. Are high and low frequency behavior percentages mentioned?
c. Are patterns mentioned and accounted for?
d. Are all inferences and generalizations supported by data? Are the data mentioned in the report?
e. Was data used to discuss one of the hypotheses?
f. Are all sentences in the report complete?

A Sample Interaction Analysis Report

The experimenter observed a college Educational Psychology recitation class of 24 students. The observation data are presented in Fig. 1. The most frequent behavior to occur was No. 5, student statements, (50 percent). The two low frequency behaviors were No. 3 and No. 4, (0 percent). The primary pattern was 5–5 ⟶ 5–1 ⟶ 1–1 ⟶ 5–5, from continued stu-

dent statements to teacher support or praise and back to student state-
ments. Two secondary patterns should be noted; 5–5 $\longrightarrow$ 5–2 $\longrightarrow$ 2–5,
student statements followed by teacher questions followed by student state-
ments and, 5–5 $\longrightarrow$ 5–7 $\longrightarrow$ 7–6 $\longrightarrow$ 6–5, which was student statements
followed by silence followed by student questions followed by student
statements. Categories involving students, No. 5 and No. 6, comprised 60
percent of the total interaction, which indicates that the class was student–
centered during this period.

The hypothesis that reinforcement of student responses by teacher
praise or support will yield a high frequency of student responses was supported by the data from this observation. Student response rate was high,
50 percent, as was teacher praise, 25 percent.

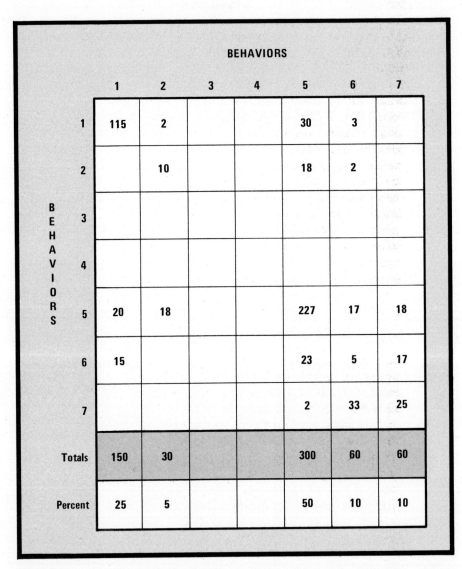

		1	2	3	4	5	6	7
	1	115	2			30	3	
	2		10			18	2	
	3							
	4							
	5	20	18			227	17	18
	6	15				23	5	17
	7					2	33	25
Totals		150	30			300	60	60
Percent		25	5			50	10	10

BEHAVIORS (columns), BEHAVIORS (rows)

Figure 6.3 Interaction Analysis Matrix for Classroom Observation No. 1 (Note to student: On the final matrix it is often more convenient to enter a single number in a cell rather than drawing in the number of tallies. This is done in the matrix above.)

♦ SUMMARY

Unit Six provided several things: an introduction to the notion that the interaction between teacher and student is important; an introduction to a method for evaluation of interaction; exposure to a way of using interaction analysis data, namely, to evaluate hypotheses; and an introduction to a statistical tool for viewing data—the matrix. Since analysis of interaction requires identification of the activities occurring, it is necessary to have activity or behavior categories. The interaction analysis scheme used in this unit employs seven different categories. The data resulting from systematic observation and recording can readily be transferred to a 7 x 7 matrix. The method for converting raw data to matrix form was explained as well as methods for evaluating matrix information.

The experience aspect of Unit Six called for observation of three different classrooms using the interaction analysis technique. The report resulting from each observation is more than just busy work; it is a means for clarifying data and organizing the information available. In addition, the student is given the opportunity to use his own data to form conclusions and attack or defend stated hypotheses.

Hopefully, there are a great many more outcomes from this unit than those listed above. The reader or student who has completed three observations should have some perplexing and disturbing questions at hand. First of all, some observers should have realized how little one sees when observation is not systematic and purposeful. Interaction analysis can train the observer to be much more accurate in his casual observations and "see" a lot more interaction when the observation is systematic. The implications of such training are obvious for the teacher who must observe as well as talk, guide, or discipline. What are other implications? Could you train elementary children to observe some activity in a systematic manner? What would you have them look for in activities like debates, or plays, or even major altercations in the classroom?

On the other hand, some observers ought to be questioning the technique. Was it reliable? Did you classify behaviors properly? How do you know? Were more categories needed? What were they? How can you adequately define a behavior category? Categories ought to be "mutually exclusive." That is, if a behavior fits into one category, it cannot fit into any other category. It is "excluded" from other categories if it fits into one. As *you* understand the seven categories used in Unit Six, are they mutually exclusive?

Further questions should be considered about the technique; for instance, do you wish to observe a classroom on this level? Are there physical interactions which must also be considered? To what extent does the interaction analysis technique contribute to your understanding of the teaching and learning process? Is it an approach which you would incorporate?

Many critics of education accuse teachers of operating on a verbal level with little emphasis on development in other areas. A teacher guilty of this practice would probably lecture as a means of transmitting information to the exclusion of other methods. Did you observe and record this type of teaching taking place? Have you experienced it from the student's position? What would you rather see happen? Why? What would be the outcome of a "teacher question–student statement–teacher praise–student question–student statement" pattern? What pattern do you plan to employ if you handle a discussion class? Studies have been completed showing that even elementary teachers use "teacher centered" strategies to *teach* rather than "learner centered" strategies for *learning*. What is the difference between teaching and learning? Does the interaction analysis technique point up any possible differences?

Once again, it is time for you to consider whether or not this psychological approach to learning and teaching has something to offer you.

♦ SUGGESTED ADDITIONAL ACTIVITIES

1. State several hypotheses about the relationship between teacher and student in different subject matter areas. For example, an hypothesis about math courses might be, "Math discussion classes will have more teacher lecture than student statements and be more teacher-centered than student-centered." From your experience you could speculate on the predominant activities in other subject matter areas. After establishing the hypotheses, observe several classes of the subject matter in question. Determine if the data supports your hypotheses. Of course, you want to be careful not to over-generalize your findings to *all* situations, but the results you achieve are an indication of what is happening in a few particular situations.

2. What do you think is the predominant activity in the first-grade class in the school nearest to you now? In the fifth grade? In the tenth grade? Is there any reason to believe that patterns of interaction should or do change from one grade level to another? You could get some data which would provide a partial answer to this question by systematically observing various classes in a school system. Your answer might be that the grade level is not the important variable. Perhaps, the subject matter is the important variable as mentioned in Suggested Additional Activity 1 above. If neither of these two variables, subject matter and grade level, is the critical influencing factor, then what is? Is it possible that many different variables act at the same time with the amount of influence changing from situation to situation? If you come to such a conclusion, then you might begin to consider what it will mean to your own performance in a classroom as a teacher or as a student.

♦ SUGGESTED ADDITIONAL READINGS

For Basic Information About Interaction Analysis

Amidon, E. J., and Flanders, N. A. "Interaction Analysis as a Feedback System." In E. J. Amidon and J. B. Hough eds. *Interaction Analysis: Theory, Research and Application.* Reading, Mass.: Addison-Wesley, 1967, pp. 121–140.

Flanders, N. A. *Teacher Influence, Pupil Attitudes, and Achievement.* Washington, D.C.: U.S. Dept. HEW, 1965.

For More Advanced Information

Amidon, E. J., and Flanders, N. A. *The Role of the Teacher in the Classroom.* Minneapolis: Amidon and Associates, 1963.

Amidon, E. J., and Hough, J. B. eds. *Interaction Analysis: Theory, Research and Application.* Reading, Mass.: Addison-Wesley, 1967.

Bales, R. F. *Interaction Process Analysis.* Reading, Mass.: Addison-Wesley, 1950.

Flanders, N. A. *Analyzing Teaching Behavior.* Reading, Mass.: Addison–Wesley, 1970.

For Specific Studies on Classroom Interaction

Amidon, E. J., and Hough, J. B. eds. *Interaction Analysis: Theory, Research and Application.* Reading, Mass.: Addison-Wesley, 1967. (In addition to giving advanced information, this book contains 28 studies in classroom interaction.)

Cogan, M. L. "Theory and Design of a Study of Teacher-pupil Interaction." *Harvard Educational Review* 26(1956):315–342.

Denny, D. A. "Identification of Teacher-Classroom Variables Facilitating Pupil Creative Growth." *American Educational Research Journal* 5(1968):365–384.

Lahaderne, Henrietta M., and Jackson, P. W. "Withdrawl in the Classroom." *Journal of Educational Psychology* 61(1970):97–101.

Lantz, D. L. "The Relationship of University Supervisors and Supervising Teachers' Ratings to Observed Student Teachers' Behavior." *American Educational Research Journal* 4(1967):279–288.

May, F. B., and DeVault, M. Vere "Hypothetical Dimensions of Teachers' Communication." *American Educational Research Journal* 4(1967):271–278.

Medley, D. M., and Mitzel, H. E. "Techniques For Measuring Classroom Behavior." *Journal of Educational Psychology* 49(1958):86–92.

UNIT 7

Behavior Management

♦ BACKGROUND

The teacher is responsible for the education of each child in a classroom. But, what is meant by "responsible for the education?" Some psychologists interpret this to mean that the teacher is responsible for the behavior changes which should occur in a classroom. For instance, reading is part of a child's education. The act of reading is behavior. Therefore, if a student is learning to read in a classroom, a behavior change is occurring. It is expected that a teacher will use the most efficient means for promoting that behavior change. It is at this point that the principles of *behavior management* must be considered. Through the careful use of reinforcement techniques, the teacher *can* manage many of the behavior changes occurring in a classroom.

The general purpose of this unit is to expose you to the basic principles of behavior management and give you the opportunity to apply them to a situational problem. As you will soon discover, behavior management encompasses many more basic concepts and operations than you encountered in previous units. In fact, it is fairly safe to say that in order to be considered fairly knowledgeable in behavior management, one should know a reasonable amount of the information available about reinforcement theory. This one unit cannot presume to achieve such lofty outcomes. But, upon completing this unit you will have a good grounding in the basic notions about reinforcement, and you will have experienced some application of the principles. In order to achieve some background information, consider the following questions:

As noted in the preface, this unit was coauthored by Dr. James Johnson, Associate Professor of Psychology, State University of New York at Plattsburgh.

209

What is the difference between "responses" and "classes of responses"?

It is often necessary for one person to evaluate another person's performance. This task permeates our environment; we look at a child's performance to determine if promotion from one grade to another is appropriate, attention is given to an employee's performance to see if promotion is warranted, an evaluation is made of a patient's behavior to determine whether discharge or continued hospitalization is indicated, and so forth. In order to evaluate a person's performance, we must attend to their responses or behaviors.

People engage in a wide variety of specific *responses*. In fact, so many discrete responses are possible that it can be very difficult keeping them in order. Therefore, we frequently find ourselves considering *classes* of responses. For example:

I. Academic responses:	II. Grooming responses:	III. Aggressive responses:
1. going to class	1. taking a shower	1. hitting another child
2. reading the text	2. brushing teeth	2. rough play in sports
3. taking notes	3. shining shoes	3. shouting at peers
4. _____	4. _____	4. _____
5. _____	5. _____	5. _____

Add two additional responses in the number 4 and 5 spots for each of the response classes. Now, decide on three more classes of responses and give five specific behaviors appropriate for each one.

IV. _____	V. _____	VI. _____
1. _____	1. _____	1. _____
2. _____	2. _____	2. _____
3. _____	3. _____	3. _____
4. _____	4. _____	4. _____
5. _____	5. _____	5. _____

Why is the difference between responses and response classes important to the educator?

An exercise such as the one above leads us to a couple of conclusions about the observation of responses. First, when we speak in terms of response classes, we are not being very precise and are not conveying as much information as possible. As was demonstrated, when we talk in terms of response classes, we encompass a wide range of specific behaviors. More effective communication would result if we observed and spoke in terms of specific responses. For example, children are often referred to a school psychologist because they appear *emotionally disturbed*. Frequently this is the only thing written on the referral. This label is supposed to communicate a picture of the child to the school psychologist. Even worse, the psychologist may perpetuate the error by assuming that he knows what is being said by the label, *emotionally disturbed*. However, if he were honest with himself, he would have to admit that the only information he has at this point is that this particular child's behavior is deviant enough in class so as to warrant the teacher's attention. From his training, he knows that the category *emotionally disturbed* encompasses a wide range of behaviors. Rarely, if ever, are all these behaviors found in one given child.

You can probably anticipate the next question from the previous exercise. What particular behaviors does this child exhibit that have drawn your attention and prompted the referral? It should become apparent that the pattern is not perfectly consistent from child to child, and that each time the label, *emotionally disturbed,* is used, we are not, in fact, referring to the same set of behaviors.

Write a simple referral which you think will convey the specific information necessary for a school psychologist to initiate a treatment program for a child, or to recommend one for a teacher to undertake.

_____

_____

_____

_____

_____

_____

_____

_____

_____

_____

To summarize the critical point of this task, it is most important to specify particular responses within a response class in order to insure accurate communication. If we say that a child will be retained in the fifth grade because he is not sixth-grade material, we are implying that this child has mastered none of the skills typically taught in the fifth grade. Once again, this is not the usual case. Being more specific, it might be said that the child is deficient in the mathematics required to progress another grade. Within mathematics his particular difficulty is working with decimals. Such specification gives a more definite target behavior toward which remedial work can be focused. Time will not be lost drilling in skills that the child has already mastered. Conversely, there will be maximum efficiency in getting the child at the appropriate level of responding in mathematics.

What is the relationship between responses and standardization of measurement?

We have spent some time talking about the observation of behavior and the importance of specification in this task. To further elaborate, let's discuss how to *describe* the behaviors we observe. Since the English vocabulary already contains so many words for describing people, one would not anticipate any problem as to which words to use. People or their activities can be labeled *wealthy, honest,* or *intelligent,* and these labels seem satisfactory for communicating the desired information in everyday conversation. This is similar to the use of the term, emotionally disturbed, in the preceding section. As was stressed at that point, a more profitable alternative would be to use terms that are more quantitatively descriptive, for example, substituting *annual income* for *wealth, IQ score* for *intelligence, school grades* for *academic inclination.*

The word *intelligence* appears to have the advantages of being applicable in a wide variety of situations and more meaningfully related to complex human performance. On the other hand, the term *IQ* is more specific. This distinction highlights the difference between two philosophies of dealing with behavior. The important difference is the extent to which each depends on the personal interpretation or judgment of the observer. The subjective measures of wealth and intelligence are greatly influenced by the observer's interpretation, whereas the objective terms, annual income and IQ score, have a standard meaning that is not greatly affected by the momentary mood of the observer.

One might ask why there is such a great need for standardization. The major reason is that it facilitates communication and assures accurate replication when desired. An observation which is affected by the personal bias of the perceiver and communicated to another is subjected to the same sort of subjective interpretation by the person who receives the communication and so on. If we communicate in standard units of measure, we can be more confident that the same perception that we *experienced* is construed by the person receiving the communication. Therefore, it is the need for replication that requires that the terms used in an observation be relatively free of personal interpretations and evaluations. As a consequence of this need for replication, the decision to use *descriptive* rather than *interpretive* terms seems more appropriate.

One final caution should be noted. People are frequently satisfied to use subjective generalizations in summarizing observations because there appears to be fairly good reliability resulting between observers. This is the fallacy of the reliability coefficient. There are at least two possible explanations for general agreement between subjective observations. First, the generalizations may be so vague so as to defy contradiction; they encompass such a wide range of possible behaviors. Second, these reliability measures may say nothing about the physical basis of the observation but may only reflect social agreement which might very well have occurred entirely on the basis of shared subjective interpretations.

This latter condition may sound acceptable to you until you think, for example, how many times and how has your subjective interpretation of the word *wealth* changed from the day you received your first allowance to the present. Let's say eight times, that is, you have had eight different definitions of wealth. At each point, you have some agreement with others about your subjective interpretation of wealth, but at the same time you were out of phase with all the others who may have been holding one of the other seven definitions.

For the following words, suggest some more objective, descriptive definitions:

Studious_____

_____

Friendly_____

_____

Trustworthy_____

_____

Trusting_____

_____

Make-up three more generalized statements and then give specific descriptions in their place.

_____

_____

_____

_____

_____

_____

_____

_____

What are rates of responses?

We have been observing responses in a descriptive manner that allows for quantification and, therefore, insures more accurate communication. Proceeding in this fashion, we notice a couple of things almost immediately; one, that any given person engages in a wide range of behaviors, and, two, that all of these behaviors do not occur with the same frequency. This may appear to be a statement of the very obvious, but this information is critically important for our later discussions.

We are saying that all behaviors occur with a certain probability. Within a given person's behavior repertoire, certain behaviors occur more frequently than others. It could be said that these more frequently occurring behaviors have a higher probability. For example, in the classroom, under ordinary conditions, talking to someone in the front of the room (the instructor) should have a higher probability than hitting the person sitting next to you.

However, we cannot quickly generalize and say that when a group of people are sitting before some person or persons it is appropriate to speak out to this person. Think, for example, of being at a play or at an invited address. An important point about the above should be highlighted: talking about *rates of behavior*, the concern is with frequency.

What is meant by "appropriate" and "inappropriate" response rates?

Very often, large segments of a person's behavior repertoire do not stand out because they occur rather routinely, that is, at appropriate rates. Conversely, of particular interest are inappropriate rates. These can be of two varieties, inappropriately high rates and inappropriately low rates. We shall call the former *behavior excesses* and the latter *behavior deficits*. Typically, one of these two conditions exist when we label a situation as abnormal, troublesome, undesirable, and so forth. It is in these situations that we attempt to effect a change.

When and how is a behavior defined as being in excess or deficient to an inappropriate degree?

It is almost redundant to say that universal standards cannot be set dictating appropriate levels of a given behavior. Our sociocultural system has assured the fact that certain classes of behaviors will be more probable among particular segments of the population than among others. Even within a given segment of the population, no numerical standards for selected behaviors can be assumed, or, for that matter, even considered desirable.

How do we bring some order to this wide-open field? To begin with, it might be stated that the frequency of a particular behavior for a particular person is usually determined by those persons in his environment who have control over the consequences of the particular behavior. This has overtones of being a social definition, and this is very appropriate. It is the interactions with those in the surrounding environment that bring consequences to bear on behaviors. In other words, for every bit of behavior there is a reaction or a consequence administered personally or programmed by some person in the environment. *These consequences affect the probability of occurrence of specific behaviors.* Therefore, a carefully programmed operation of consequences will effect a desired change in frequency in the target behavior. These operations will be the focus of our attention in the next several sections.

As a task at this point, choose four specific behaviors and for each one name a situation in which a high rate of the behavior would be appropriate, and the situation in which a high rate would be undesirable for the same behavior. A sample is already done for you.

	Specific Behavior	High Rate Desirable	High Rate Undesirable
1.	Running————	On running track———	In school hallway———
2.			
3.			
4.			
5.			

Now, do the same for specific behaviors and low rates of occurrence.

	Specific Behavior	Low Rate Desirable	Low Rate Undesirable
1.			
2.			
3.			
4.			
5.			

Finally, analyze your own working environment and list those behaviors of your own that are appropriate at high rates and those that should have low rates.

High Rates	Low Rates

Now, do the same for the behaviors of those you come in contact with, for example, students, patients, or employees.

High Rates	Low Rates

What are the major steps involved in changing rates of behavior?

You may note the title of this section and be elated that we are finally getting to the apparent heart of behavior management, that is, changing the rate of a behavior. Well, we are almost there, but first there are several crucial points which deserve further attention. There are three steps which are critical aspects of any behavior modification program. These steps are:

1. Analyzing the situation to specify the behavior to be changed

2. Finding the consequences which are maintaining the current behavior

3. Discovering which consequences may be manipulated in order to change the rate of behavior

In number one, we are recording what is referred to as a *baseline*. A *baseline* or *base rate* is the frequency of occurrence of a given behavior under usual environmental conditions, that is, before we change any of the consequences of the behavior. This baseline should be observed over several days until we see some orderliness in the behavior pattern. The purpose of establishing the base rate is to give us a precise starting point from which we can make comparisons after the modification program has been initiated.

An example of establishing a base rate would be the situation in which people wish to reduce the number of cigarettes they smoke. When asked how many cigarettes a person smokes now, the usual answer is something like, "a pack or two a day." This is not sufficiently precise since it allows for a range of 20 cigarettes, from one pack (20) to two packs (40) without any discrimination. This particular person may make a concerted effort to stop smoking and smoke only one pack per day for three days. But, this is not discriminately different from the description of the initial rate and does not show marked progress. This lack of progress may be discouraging and be sufficient reason for the person to drop the program.

On the other hand, if this person had taken a precise count (baseline) for three to five days, he would know his exact rate of cigarette smoking. Suppose it averaged 35 per day; then a reduction to 20 would signal significant progress for the program.

In each case below, check off the series of numbers which you think is an adequate baseline for a given behavior and state the reason for your choice. Remember, it is the trend of the numbers which is important, not the absolute values. If you have difficulty deciding upon one, try placing the values on a graph.

1. _____16, 18, 18, 19, 17, 15, 16

   _____16, 19, 14, 19, 15, 23, 13

   _____

   _____

2. _____14, 15, 15, 16, 17, 18, 19

   _____15, 13, 19, 14, 20, 16, 18

   _____

   _____

3. _____13, 14, 15, 13, 14, 15, 13

   _____16, 13, 15, 17, 14, 13, 16

   _____

   _____

How do you find the consequences which maintain the current behavior?

While observing and recording the baseline for a particular behavior, you should be particularly sensitive to any events which accompany the occurrence of the behavior. We are now dealing with Step 2, finding the consequences which are maintaining the current behavior. This is, at times, a particularly difficult task, since these consequences are sometimes quite subtle or arise from unexpected sources. Obviously, very careful attention should be given to those persons being observed. This includes the observer.

In many cases of undesirable behaviors, the consequences maintaining the behavior are not readily observable. That is why the occurrence of these behaviors is so puzzling to us. Part of the problem here is that we tend to look at the situation from our own personal perspective, and if we don't perceive anything in the environment which we consider to be a desirable consequence, we don't understand what could be maintaining a given behavior in another person. This, once again, emphasizes the need for objectivity in our observations.

There are some questions that we can ask ourselves to guide our observations. Some of these questions are:

1. What are the reactions of the people around the person when he engages in the behavior?
2. What are my reactions on these occasions?
3. What conditions are prevailing in the environment of the person at the time of his behavior?
4. How are these conditions changed after the behavior has occurred?

The goal here is to find a consistency in the answer to some of these questions from one occurrence of the behavior to the next.

What is meant by "manipulating consequences"?

We can now turn to the last point, that is, discovering how the consequences may be manipulated in order to change the rate of the behavior. We are attempting here to restructure the contingency in such a way that a more acceptable rate of behavior will result. Depending on the behavior in question, we will be looking for an increase or decrease in the rate. This will involve modifying the environmental consequence in some way through the use of either positive or negative reinforcement. The most important question here is, what can I do or arrange to have others do in order to obtain a more acceptable response from the person being observed?

What is the relationship between increasing the rate of behavior and positive reinforcement?

Having observed and recorded baseline of the target behavior, we have seen that sometimes the goal is to increase the frequency of that behavior over its baseline rate. This goal, in fact, defines positive reinforcement. It is a consequence of a behavior which serves to increase the probability that the same behavior will occur again. For example, if upon meeting someone for the first time, there is a pleasant interaction, the probability is higher that you seek out the companionship of that person in the future. Here, the pleasant exchange between the two of you has reinforced the behavior of spending time together.

When might positive reinforcement be used?

There are several different occasions in which positive reinforcement would be most appropriately used. The goal in each situation would be the same (increase the rate of a behavior), however, the starting point is different in each case. The first situation would be the condition in which the behavior rate is already at an acceptable level. The primary purpose here would be to establish conditions which would assure the maintenance of the desirable rate and possibly even increase it further. An example of this might be the study behaviors of a child. He already studies enough to maintain an average which is acceptable to you. However, you want to be very sure you know what precise consequences are maintaining this study output so that you can continue to be consistent to the application of these consequences. So, the main purpose here is the clarification of existing contingencies to maintain ongoing behaviors. If there is some further increase in the rate of the behavior as a result of this clarification, that would be a very acceptable situation.

Another occasion calling for the use of positive reinforcement would be when it is desirable to increase the rate of an already existing behavior. In such situations, there is obviously some positive reinforcement contingency in effect, since the behavior is already occurring. The problem here appears to be that the reinforcement is not as effective as it might be. There could be a number of factors accounting for this. First, the reinforcer being used to maintain the behavior may not be the most effective for this particular person. A second possibility is that the reinforcement is not delivered frequently enough. This would serve to keep the behavior at a low rate. The third possibility is that the reinforcement is not of sufficient size or magnitude when it is presented.

All of these three points can be summarized by saying that the overall consequence of the behavior is not strong enough for the person to engage in the behavior very frequently. It might be concluded that if there is an alternative available, the person is more likely to perform the alternative behavior. It is on those occasions when conditions are not appropriate for an alternative response that the person will engage in the specified response.

The third situation calling for the administration of positive reinforcement would be an instance in which it is desirable to establish a new behavior in a person's repertoire. In this case the baseline rate of the target behavior would be zero. However, when establishing a new behavior, it would probably be a painstaking and futile task to wait for the behavior to occur in its final form before we administer a reinforcement. Since these behaviors have not occurred up to the present, there is no reason to suspect that the person will spontaneously emit the specified behavior.

How is "shaping" related to the situation in which a new behavior is to be established?

Essentially, shaping is a procedure in which good approximations of the desired response are reinforced. As the process progresses, the requirement to obtain the reinforcement becomes more and more stringent until finally the target behavior is obtained.

The rationale behind the shaping procedure is that a response is never totally new. The person already has many of the component parts of the target behavior in his repertoire. The purpose of shaping is to reorganize these various components into the proper sequence. For example, even before they look at a typewriter for the first time, most people already have full command of all the physical movements found in typing. The instruction (shaping) process is therefore simply one of structuring and sequencing these physical events into a chain of behaviors that is called typing.

Once the behavior is established in this way, it is then maintained over time under a regime of positive reinforcement.

What is "reinforcement sampling"?

There are some additional points which should be included in background material. As was seen in the paragraphs above, there are occasions when a behavior is kept at a low rate because the reinforcer being used is not the most effective for that person. With a bit of prior planning, such a situation can be readily circumvented. The solution is simply to discover what are the effective reinforcers for a given person. One way to obtain this information is to ask the person. However, a more empirical answer can be obtained by observing the person and noting those reinforcers for which they will work regularly. This procedure is known as *reinforcement sampling*.

What is a "reinforcement hierarchy"?

Now that it is known what the effective reinforcers are for a person, they should be placed in some order of preference. Obviously, all cannot be valued to an equal degree. For example, would most six-year-olds value "teacher praise" as highly as candy, or toy trucks? A *reinforcement hierarchy* is now being established. At the onset of training it is wise to use the most effective reinforcer, but as time passes, a lag in responding may be noted. It might be that the person has become *satiated* with the reinforcer being used. When satiation develops, it is most expedient to have the next preferred reinforcer available in order to maintain the desired rate of response. Another approach is to intermingle the three or four preferred reinforcers from the onset of training, therefore reducing the probability of satiation for any of them.

Are behavioral procedures "mechanical" and "artificial"?

One final point needs emphasis. A common complaint and argument against the use of behavior procedures in the classroom is that it is mechanical and artificial. In some cases, this has probably been a justified complaint. Behavior situations can be made to appear very artificial. However, this need not be the case nor is it desirable. The point is that there are a wealth of stimulus events in the regular classroom procedure that can be used as reinforcers if they are programmed as such and administered appropriately.

Use these stimuli! As it is, they are maintaining some kind of behavior; you may as well make them contingent upon appropriate behaviors. In addition to avoiding artificiality, reorganizing the existing structure will also save the expense of introducing new reinforcers and avoid the problems of administrative authorization.

Name three common behavior deficits that you are confronted with in the classroom.

_____

_____

_____

Choose the one of the above which has the lowest or zero rate. Specify the target behavior and then name the successive approximations of this behavior that you would reinforce during the shaping process.

Target behavior:_____

Approximations:_____

_____

_____

_____

_____

Name five potential positive reinforcers that currently exist in your classroom situation.

_____

_____

_____

_____

_____

How does one decrease rates of behavior by "extinction"?

As was noted in an earlier section, there are occasions when the rate of a specified behavior is inappropriately high. There are a number of possible methods used to reduce the rate of these behavior excesses. One of the more apparent procedures is to remove the positive reinforcement which is currently maintaining the behavior. This process is known as *extinction*. Just as the administration of positive reinforcement was instrumental in building up the behavior, the removal of it should be effective in reducing the frequency. Essentially, you have removed the payoff for the person's performance of the response.

There are several factors which will influence how long it takes for extinction to occur. The most readily apparent is the amount of positive reinforcement the person has previously received for the behavior. If it is a behavior which has been maintained for a number of years, extinction will be a slow process since the behavior is probably very firmly established.

Also, if the person has been engaged in this response for an extended period of time, it is most likely that he was not reinforced for it on every single occasion. That is, there were probably instances of non-reinforcement for the behavior. Since extinction is simply a period of extended non-reinforcement, it may take the person a while to discriminate the current extinction condition from a period of non-reinforcement in his previous history.

So, in order to use extinction effectively, it is imperative that one remove all the possible reinforcers for the specified behavior, and that they are withdrawn consistently. If there is a lapse in the procedure and the person is accidentally reinforced for the specified behavior during extinction, the behavior will continue to occur that much longer.

What is meant by "punishment"?

Another procedure used to diminish the rate of behavior is *punishment*. Punishment is an aversive stimulus administered consequent to a behavior. This aversive stimulus is presented after each occurrence of the behavior. The rationale for punishment is that the person will no longer perform the response if this undesirable event is the only result. Potential punishers range from physical events such as a shock or slap to verbal censure. An important thing to remember about punishment is that it is defined by its effect on a behavior. Punishing stimuli cannot be universally defined, that is, no matter how a person perceives a stimulus, it cannot be defined as a punisher unless it suppresses a particular behavior.

Punishment is most often used in those situations in which it is imperative to terminate a response rapidly. This process is much quicker than the extinction process.

A final point to consider when using punishment to suppress a behavior; it is recommended that an alternative behavior be positively reinforced at the same time that punishment occurs. This will allow the desirable alternative to fill the behavioral void of the punished response.

Name some inappropriate classroom behaviors that can be handled by extinction.

_____

_____

_____

Name some that might require the use of punishment.

_____

_____

_____

In order to complete the experience part of this unit, it is necessary for you to be familiar with a variety of "behavior modification" terms. The following questions will help you with those terms:

What is a positive reinforcer?

This was discussed earlier under the question, What is the relationship between increasing the rate of behavior and positive reinforcement? It is a consequence of a behavior which serves to increase the probability that the same behavior will occur again.

What is negative reinforcement?

This was not discussed in any of the earlier questions. It is the disappearance of an aversive stimulus as a consequence of a response. It is necessary that the response which removed the aversive stimulus increase in frequency in order to claim that negative reinforcement has occurred. An example of negative reinforcement would be a situation in which child A runs away from child B, when child B pinches. If the pinch is an aversive stimulus and "running away" increases in frequency when the aversive stimulus is present, then "running away" as a response is probably negatively reinforcing.

What is a conditioned reinforcer?

This was not discussed in any of the earlier questions. A conditioned reinforcer is a neutral stimulus which acquires the properties of a reinforcer through the process of pairing it with a reinforcer.

What is extinction?

This was discussed under the question, How does one decrease rates of behavior by extinction? It is the process in which frequency of a response deceases when all possible reinforcers for that response are withdrawn.

What is punishment?

This was discussed earlier under the question, What is meant by punishment? Punishment is an aversive stimulus administered consequent to a behavior which results in a decrease in the frequency of that behavior.

What is meant by shaping?

This was discussed under the question, How is shaping related to the situation in which a new behavior is to be established? Shaping is the reinforcement of good approximations to the final, desired response.

What is meant by "baseline"?

This was discussed earlier under the question, What are the major steps involved in changing rates of behavior? A baseline or base rate is the frequency of occurrence of a given behavior under usual environmental conditions; that is, before we change any of the consequences of the behavior.

What is meant by a "reinforcement contingency"?

This was not specifically discussed in any of the earlier questions, but only mentioned briefly. A contingency is the condition required for reinforcement or punishment to occur. For example, a child might receive praise only if he picks up his toys. The reinforcement, praise, is contingent upon a specific behavior, namely, picking up toys.

It is time to apply some of what you know about behavior management to an experience.

♦ AN EXPERIENCE

*How is the experience part of this unit different from the others
you have encountered?*

The basic purpose of an experience in a learning situation is to expose the learner to commonplace phenomena and variables. In other units the experiences called for real people, classrooms, teachers, and students, but in this unit a different strategy will be used. Here is the reason for a different strategy: Behavior management or modification involves changing the behavior of another human being which is fine if the person manipulating the behavior is in a position of authority and responsibility. We cannot be assured that every reader has the authority and responsibility for managing another human's behavior. Therefore, the author of this book cannot suggest that you go out into the community and begin changing behaviors.

We can, however, employ a technique that many applied learning theorists have found to be successful. We will use the concept of *simulation*. If the learner cannot be placed in the real situation, the teacher puts him in a situation which has most of the characteristics of the real situation, that is, a simulation of reality. We are assuming that you cannot yet operate with behavior management in a real classroom. How about a simulated classroom? A close simulation of a real classroom would be one in which the students played certain roles, or simply acted. It is obvious that such a setting is impossible for a textbook to achieve. A simulation somewhat further from the real case, but still workable would be one in which the students are described in writing, and the person managing the behavior operates with that written description. A written description simulation will be used with this unit. On the next few pages is a description of Elmwood Educational Facility and a student at Elmwood named John. You are to design behavior management strategies which you would use with John.

What is Elmwood Educational Facility like?

Elmwood Educational Facility is part of a Learning Disabilities Center. The students in the Basic Level Area have been diagnosed as having disabilities which prevent them from learning basic skills such as reading, writing, and math. Materials for each of these skills are available in small rooms set off the main activities room (see Fig. 7.1). The materials have been tested and shown to work for students like those assigned to Elmwood.

John attends Elmwood. He cannot read, write (even single letters), or count. He spends about 60 percent of each period at point A in Fig. 7.1 and 40 percent at point B. There are desks at both places. He will move from A to

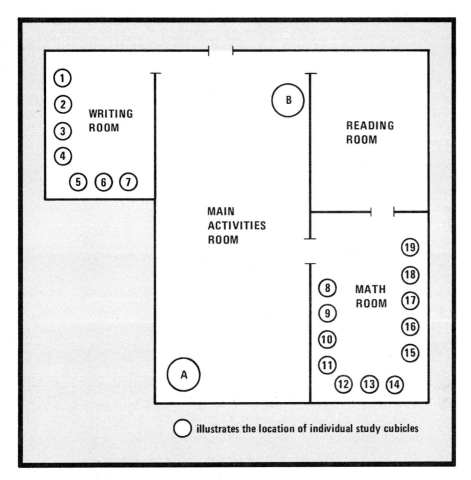

Figure 7.1 Floor-plan of the Elmwood Educational Facility.

B and back about once every 10 minutes. Obviously, his response rates on math, reading, and writing materials are zero. (He must enter one of the rooms to be exposed to the materials.)

The materials in the Basic Skills Rooms are constructed so that small, simple responses can be made by the student and observed and/or reinforced by the teacher.

Small pieces of candy will work as reinforcers for John. Neither praise, encouragement, nor attention from the teacher have operated as reinforcers in the past. John seems to ignore the teacher at all times. Directions appear to be not heard and, certainly, not followed.

Experience Objectives

Your tasks in this experience are to:

1. Describe the shaping process you would use to get John from the Main Activities Room into a Basic Skills Room.

2. Describe the shaping process you would use to increase John's response rate with the Basic Skills materials.

3. Describe the shaping process you would use to get John from one Basic Skills Room into another—and working.

4. Describe the process of establishing the teacher as an agent for dispensing conditioned reinforcers.

5. After you have completed the tasks above, generate some hypothetical data to show John's response rates for various activities. Place this data on Fig. 7.2.

As you change reinforcers or change the response which will be reinforced, make certain that you draw a vertical line on the graph and identify the nature of that period—just as has already been done with the baseline period.

Suggested Procedure for Achieving the Experience Objectives

1. Identify and list the approximations of behavior necessary to shape John from the Main Activities Room into the Basic Skills Room. Identify the reinforcers you would use, and when you would use them.

2. Identify and list the approximations necessary to shape an increase in response rate with instructional materials. Identify the reinforcers you would use, and when they would be used.

3. Identify and list the approximations you would reinforce to get John from one Basic Skills Room into another. Identify the reinforcers used, and time when they are used.

4. Identify the conditioned reinforcers you would like to establish. Identify and list the steps you would use to establish the conditioned reinforcers.

5. Coordinate the shaping phases listed in 1, 2, 3, and 4 above with the graph in Fig. 7.2, and prepare some hypothetical data for the graph.

6. Prepare a written description of the actions taken in 1, 2, 3, and 4 above.

7. Compare your written description with the Situational Problem Report Guidelines Sheet.

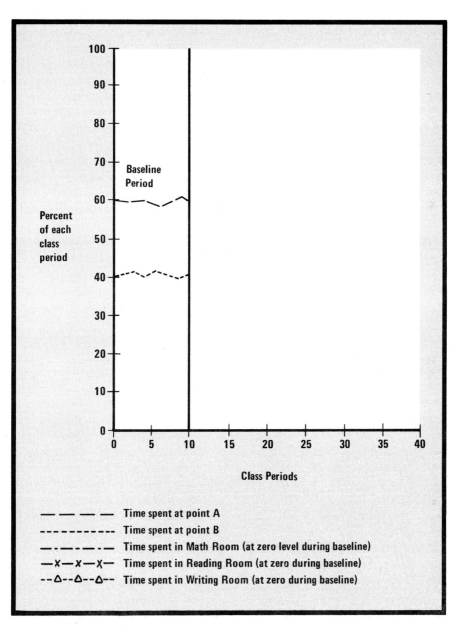

Figure 7.2 Graph illustrating percent of time spent by John in various locations within the Elmwood Educational Facility

Progress Chart

Activity	Check each space when completed.
1. Behavioral approximations: John from Main to Basic Skills Room	_____
Reinforcers	_____
Time of reinforcement	_____
2. Behavioral approximations: Increase in response rates	_____
Reinforcers	_____
Time of reinforcement	_____
3. Behavioral approximations: John from Basic Skills Rooms	_____
Reinforcers	_____
Time of reinforcement	_____
4. Identification of conditioned reinforcers	_____
Steps	_____
5. Place hypothetical data on graph	_____
6. Write report	_____
7. Compare report to guidelines	_____

Situational Problem Report Guidelines Sheet

All of the following items should be included in your Situational Problem Report:

1. Specify all contingencies clearly.
2. Specify the response desired. Don't use a response class description.
3. Specify the attempted reinforcer.
4. Specify the anticipated approximations to the final, desired behavior which will be reinforced.
5. Specify the sequence in which the various contingencies and approximations will occur.
6. Identify the following processes if they occur:

   a. Shaping
   b. Extinction
   c. Positive reinforcement
   d. Negative reinforcement
   e. Punishment

   (This can be done most easily by labeling parts of the graph in Fig. 7.2.)
7. Write the report in third person.

♦ SUMMARY

The topic covered in this unit is sometimes called "behavior modification" or "operant psychology." Regardless of its title, it is a more complex and encompassing area of psychology than any of the previous units. It was the purpose of this unit to expose the reader to some of the basic concepts, operations, and principles. Below is a list of some of the areas covered in this unit:

Identification of response classes
Specification of responses within classes
Production of referral statements using response specifications
Production of behavioral definitions
Identification of behavioral deficits
Identification of behavioral excesses
Identification of behavior baselines
Identification of target behaviors
Identification of behavioral approximations to target behaviors
Identification of potential positive reinforcers
Identification of inappropriate classroom behaviors
Identification of suitable conditions for extinction procedures

Psychologists who employ a behavior management approach to educational problems are usually proficient in the skills listed above. Should the reader wish to incorporate such an approach into his teaching/learning repertoire, the basic skills listed above would permit initial steps in that direction.

A simulated classroom problem was used as the media for the experience in this unit. Without proper responsibility and authority it is probably not prudent for the novice psychologist to attempt manipulation of another person's behavior; therefore, it was suggested that the problems of behavior management be worked out on a simulated level. The reader was given the opportunity to consider a learning disability/behavior problem case and to develop contingency statements as well as behavioral analyses. It was expected that the reader would generate hypothetical data which could be placed on a graph similar to those seen in formal research reports.

Application of any large body of principles, operations, or concepts brings out many of the problems, benefits, or inconsistencies existing in the information. Application on a simulated level achieves the same end, but perhaps not as dramatically. You should be evaluating your experience at this time while still questioning whether or not you may adopt the behavior management approach as a classroom strategy. What were the various problems you encountered?

Does the notion of manipulating someone else's behavior violate your system of values or your philosophy of learning? Why? If "teaching" is a purposeful activity, then certain outcomes should result. If behavior management techniques produce those outcomes in a more consistent and efficient way than other techniques, why not use it? Have you considered what your role as a "teacher" will be? Will it be purposeful? How do local school boards and parents view the teacher's role? It seems possible to maintain that teaching is purposeful, but the purpose is not to manipulate and control behavior. Then what is the purpose? Can you measure alternative purposes if they are non-behavioral? Can the measurements be graphed for display or reporting? If you can't measure a purpose, can you claim that you have achieved that purpose? Just as in the earlier chapters, the author is giving more questions than answers. But, these questions are often best answered by the individual, and not by the professor. You might discover that your commitment to the use of behavior management techniques will depend upon the degree to which you resolve some of the questions presented in this Summary.

A further question for you to consider is, Are contingencies operating constantly, so that if they aren't managed by the teacher, they will operate on a random and, perhaps, damaging schedule? This is an argument often used in defense of behavior management. Obviously, human beings do many things for many reasons. Are the things we do (responses) the result of some prior cause (stimulus)? Or are they done because of the consequence (reinforcement)? Why do you do things? What do you expect will be the consequence of reading this book and doing the experiences? Is your behavior being controlled? Will you receive positive reinforcement as a result of the behavior you are now performing? Or are you doing it to avoid aversive stimuli (negative reinforcement)? Why *does* the average American child go to school?

Finally, if you do use behavior management techniques in your activities, what problems can you anticipate? There are many difficulties that behavioral psychologists have consistently encountered. For example, the definition and recording of practical, day-to-day, non-laboratory responses is often a perplexing and seemingly impossible task. Another problem can be the analysis of the desired behavior. The question a psychologist faces during behavioral or task analysis is, What are the appropriate approximations to reinforce? Consider the behavior of "asking meaningful questions." Just what is a "meaningful question"? It certainly sounds like something we would like to see seven-year-old children doing, but how would we know they are doing it? And what are the approximations to such a final behavior? Don't despair!! With some time and effort you could generate an adequate definition of what a question is, and what the approximations are to "asking a question." With a bit more time and considerably more effort you could define "meaningful" so that it could be applied to questions and measured. The author would hope that no one would avoid using a particular approach to learning or teaching because it required extensive time and effort. Behavior management is an approach which many psychologists and teachers have utilized with remarkable success, and as such, it deserves your attention as a possible psychological approach for you to adopt.

♦ A SUGGESTED ADDITIONAL ACTIVITY

Although it was suggested that the reader is probably not in a position to manage or change someone else's behavior through the use of behavioral techniques, it was not suggested that you should not consider managing your own behavior. There are undoubtedly some activities which you enjoy doing which are special things for you. These are possible reinforcing events. The very fact that you like to do them suggests their potential or real reinforcing qualities. Consider doing this: (1) Identify some special activity which is readily available to you, and which you would like to engage in at almost any time, (2) Identify a low frequency behavior which you would like to engage in at a more regular rate, for example, reading the classics, writing letters, or studying in the library, (3) Identify the maximum level at which you would like to eventually be performing the behavior stated in 2 above, (4) Identify the approximations to that eventual level, (5) State the contingencies which will exist at each approximation level, i.e., "I will do X amount of Y (the behavior in 2 above) before I may do Z (the behavior identified in 1 above.) If you state the contingencies and actually follow the conditions, you will be controlling or managing your own behavior. It has been suggested by psychologists that humans do not typically manage their behavior in this way; that is, we drink beer when we want, we play handball whenever the time is available, we eat lavishly whenever the opportunity presents itself. After maintaining a management regime for several weeks, begin to consider if you are imposing self-discipline or self-control. Are you controlling the behaviors you perform? How many are you actually controlling? What percent? How about the remaining behaviors? What or who controls those? How much of what you do is geared toward future reinforcement? Money in the future? How much of the total behavior in a society such as that in the United States is controlled by the token or secondary reinforcer we call "money"? Contrast that to a more "primitive" culture where a monetary exchange system does not exist. What impact would each of these systems have on education?

♦ SUGGESTED ADDITIONAL READINGS

For Basic Information on Behavior Management and Operant Psychology

Bijou, S., and Baer, D. M. *Child Development I and II.* New York: Appleton-Century Crofts, 1961.

Homme, L. *How to Use Contingency Contracting in the Classroom.* Champaign, Illinois: Research Press, 1961.

Reynolds, G. S. *A Primer of Operant Conditioning.* Glenview, Illinois: Scott, Foresman and Company, 1968.

Wenrich, W. W. *A Primer of Behavior Modification.* Belmont, California: Brooks-Cole Publishing Company, 1970.

For More Advanced Information

Ferster, C. H., and Perrott, Mary C. *Behavior Principles.* New York: Appleton-Century Crofts, 1968.

Skinner, B. F. *The Technology of Teaching.* New York: Appleton-Century Crofts, 1968.

Skinner, B. F. *Science and Human Behavior.* New York: The Macmillan Company, 1953.

Sloane, H. N. Jr., and MacAulay, Barbara D. *Operant Procedures in Remedial Speech and Language Training.* Boston: Houghton-Mifflin Company, 1968.

Ulrich, R.; Stachnik, T.; and Mabry, J. *Control of Human Behavior, Volumes One and Two.* Glenview, Illinois: Scott, Foresman and Company, 1970.

For Specific Articles

Benowitz, M. L., and Busse, R. V. "Material Incentives and the Learning of Spelling Words in a Typical School Situation." *Journal of Educational Psychology* 61(1970):24–26.

Bijou, S. W. "What Psychology has to Offer Education—Now." *Journal of Applied Behavior Analysis* 3(1970)65–71.

Cantrell, R. P.; Cantrell, Mary Lynn; Huddleston, C. M.; and Woolridge, R. L. "Contingency Contracting With School Problems." *Journal of Applied Behavior Analysis* 2(1969):215–220.

Clark, C. A., and Walberg, H. J. "The Influence of Massive Rewards on Reading Achievement in Potential Urban School Dropouts." *American Educational Research Journal* 3(1968):305–310.

Glynn, E. L. "Classroom Application of Self-Determined Reinforcement." *Journal of Applied Behavior Analysis* 3(1970):123–132.

Gray, B. B.; Baker, R. D.; and Stancyk, Susan E. "Performance Determined Instruction for Training in Remedial Reading." *Journal of Applied Behavior Analysis* 2(1969):255–264.

Hall, R. V.; Lund, Diane; and Jackson, Deloris, "Effects of Teacher Attention on Study Behavior." *Journal of Applied Behavior Analysis* 1(1968):1–12.

Hall, R. V.; Panyan, Marion; Rabon, Deloris; and Broden, Marcia. "Instructing Beginning Teachers in Reinforcement Procedures Which Improve Classroom Control." *Journal of Applied Behavior Analysis* 1(1968):315–322.

Madsen, C. H. Jr.; Becker, W. C.; and Thomas, D. R. "Rules, Praise, and Ignoring: Elements of Elementary Classroom Control." *Journal of Applied Behavior Analysis* 1(1968):139–150.

O'Leary, K. D.; Becker, W. C.; Evans, M. B.; and Saudargas, R. A. "A Token Reinforcement Program in a Public School: A Replication and Systematic Analysis." *Journal of Applied Behavior Analysis* 1(1969):3–13.

Surratt, P. R.; Ulrich, R. E.; and Hawkins, R. P. "An Elementary Student as a Behavioral Engineer." *Journal of Applied Behavior Analysis* 2(1969):85–92.

Walls, R. T. and Smith, Tennie S. "Development of Preference for Delayed Reinforcement in Disadvantaged Children." *Journal of Educational Psychology* 61(1970):118–123.

UNIT 8

Information Theory—Feedback

♦ BACKGROUND

The technological revolution which has produced the mighty rockets to carry man and machines to the planets has also produced many domestic advances that we can see daily, the computer, the color television, the cassette tape recorder—just to name a few. In addition it has increased interest in the area of human communications and, specifically, in information theory as it relates to human behavior. Machines transmit information to either man or other machines in certain limited ways. These same machines have limitations on how fast they can retrieve information from memory storage, how accurately they can reproduce information, etc. Man has many of these same limitations with precisely the same media—information. Many educators and psychologists have considered the question, How much is man like a machine in the way he processes, stores, evaluates, and does other things with information? The purpose for answering such a question is not to turn man into a machine, but to use a machine as a simple simulation of man. The simulation is considerably less complex, and, perhaps, more readily evaluated than is the real object of study—man.

So the information theory approach to learning and teaching which you will experience in this unit deals both with human behavior and with an analysis associated with the awesome technology developed by humans. It offers the teacher a reasonably scientific and quite contemporary way of looking at the educational process. This unit considers only a single area of application, information feedback. The experience permits you to employ mechanisms of information feedback. The following questions should provide the necessary background to make your experience with feedback mechanisms meaningful.

239

What is feedback?

There are many different perceptions and misperceptions about the nature and definition of feedback. Feedback means something very different to the physiological psychologist, to the information theorist, the business executive, or to the elementary school teacher. A common feature, however, in the majority of the definitions is the similarity between feedback and information, that is, feedback and information seem to be the same thing.

From a cybernetic standpoint, feedback is generally regarded as information coming to a control center pertaining to responses or events over which the center has control. For example, if a computer controlled the operation of probing arms or clamps, and if sensors in the arms relayed information back to the computer about the location of the arms, that information would be regarded as feedback.

On the other hand, the physiological psychologist typically defines feedback as those nerve impulses traveling from the peripheral receptors to the central nervous system. Impulses such as these would be used to control motor responses and similar processes. This viewpoint has often been compared with the cybernetic position. That is, the brain is the central computer, the arms are the probing appendages which send back information in the form of nerve impulses which in turn are used by the central control system to modify the action of the arms.

The major difference between the cybernetic and the physiological definitions can best be seen in Fitts and Posner's[1] description of two types of feedback, intrinsic and augmented. Both are considered to be information arising as a consequence of the organism's response, but intrinsic corresponds to the physiological definition, while augmented is information usually coming from an external agent and appears to be similar to the definition used by information theorists.

In order to clarify our usage of the term, throughout the remainder of this discussion the term "feedback" will refer to "augmented feedback." Modifications in the behavior of man and machine can arise as a result of mechanisms supplying augmented feedback to the man or the machine.

For the purpose of further clarification, we will regard feedback as information coming from an outside source to the system or organism which is or can be used to modify subsequent responses of the system. More plainly stated, feedback will be information coming to the individual about ongoing or past behaviors which is used by the individual to alter subsequent behavior. Thus, feedback is information which allows an individual to monitor his own behavior.

1. P. M. Fitts and M. I. Posner, *Human Performance* (Belmont, Calif.: Brooks/Cole Publishing Comp., 1968).

How is feedback related to information and uncertainty?

Now that we have equated feedback and information, it becomes necessary to define the term, information. It is being used here in the same sense as it was used by Shannon and Weaver,[2] who constructed a method for measuring communication. According to their theory, information contained in communication can be quantified in terms of the amount of disorganization, entropy, or "uncertainty" involved. Although this is basically a mathematical method, we will not emphasize the computational aspect here. Suffice to say that the amount of information communicated is directly related to the amount of uncertainty.

As an example of how uncertainty can be measured, let us consider a situation in which a child with a learning disability is asked to tell us what he did at time X in a classroom. If he cannot remember what behavior he was performing at point X in time, then he would have to guess in order to answer. His uncertainty would be considered quite high, given this task.

Let us assume that there are only five behaviors which he would possibly have engaged in at that moment.

His chances of guessing the correct behavior occurring are 1 in 5 if each behavior was equally probable.

Let us now assume that we have tabulated the frequency of occurrence of the five behaviors over a long period of time, and we know that the probability of behavior No. 5 occurring is, in fact, not equal to the others, but very much lower. If we communicate this to the child, we have in effect said, "Don't consider behavior No. 5 as a possibility as seriously as the others." By saying this we have decreased the number of probable behaviors and also decreased the child's uncertainty about which behavior to choose, i.e., his chances now approach 1 in 4.

The disorganization or entropy of the child as a system given this task is reflected in the number of wrong guesses which could be made. Initially, the child could have been wrong 4 out of 5 times. After being given some data about frequencies of behavior, the child came closer to possibly being wrong only 3 out of 4 times. The child became more organized, i.e., had less uncertainty. It is in this sense that feedback plays an important role. If the child could identify exactly what behavior was being performed at point X, there would be no uncertainty, hence no information to feed-back. This is the goal of augmented feedback mechanisms; to reduce uncertainty regarding the quality, type, amount, and/or sequence of behaviors occuring at a point in time or during a time span. It is only when an individual knows what behaviors he is performing, that is, he has no uncertainty about his activity,

2. C. E. Shannon and W. Weaver, *The Mathematical Theory of Communication* (Urbana, Ill.: University of Illinois Press, 1949).

that he will be able to monitor or control his behavior. Information is fed back to the organism in order to keep that uncertainty low.

Give an example of how feedback can be used.

The following hypothetical example of the use of feedback is offered as an operational definition or model which will hopefully give the reader a concrete instance from which to reason.

Imagine a ship or, rather, a Polynesian-type canoe sailing across an expanse of ocean, heading for a distant island. Imagine also that there are no landmarks, no stars or other celestial bodies, no currents, and no winds. The crew receives no information about their location whatsoever. Physiological orienting mechanisms like vision would keep them on course for a very short period of time—at least while the home island was visible. But, then, the oarsmen with the more powerful stroke would turn the canoe away from their side, the irregularities in the hull would alter the path of the vessel and soon the canoe would be hopelessly lost.

Imagine, now, that a benevolent deity places a stable star in the heavens, much like the familiar North Star of our night sky. Imagine, also that sailing straight toward the star will deliver the canoe to the target island. By placing a stick upright from the bow of the canoe, the helmsman can keep the boat on course. That is, each time he looks at the stick and the star he receives information which he can use to alter his subsequent behavior, or he receives feedback about how he has been steering the boat, and what he needs to do to correctly steer it.

How is "interval of measurement" related to behavior and feedback?

It is obvious that a more efficient system of obtaining feedback about his progress could be developed. Given the above system, he would spend a considerable amount of time off course. What might happen if he looked at the stick and the star only in the early evening and just before dawn? He would wander a great distance off course between those two times. He would come closer to the target if he checked each hour. In fact, an almost ideal system could be approached by using constant feedback monitored by a computer, such as exists in homing devices of aircraft. The point to note here is that the interval of measurement is an important variable in feedback. Shorter intervals provide less opportunity for incorrect or unwanted behavior because uncertainty is kept constantly at a low level.

What is "specificity" of information?

The preciseness or specificity of the information fed back to the control center is also an important variable. Suppose our canoe in the last example had a feedback mechanism which gave information to the helmsman constantly but in the form of comments like, "You're a little off target," or "No . . . not that direction." Our helmsman would still have difficulty monitoring his "steering behavior" given that augmented feedback. Now, suppose we calibrate into discrete units the space on each side of the stick mounted in the bow of the canoe, and we label each side of the canoe; the right being starboard, the left being port. The information fed back to the helmsman can now be very precise, i.e., "2 units to port." The discreteness or precision of the response measured is a critical variable in the construction of feedback mechanisms along with feedback interval.

Viewing the canoe transportation problem in retrospect, it can be said that traveling from island A to island B was a problem because the helmsman's rate of "on-target" responses was low relative to "off-target" responses. That is, he was more often making unproductive than productive responses. Given augmented feedback his "on-target" response rate increases and traveling from island A to island B is no longer as much of a problem.

What is a feedback mechanism?

Any formal arrangement for transmitting objective data to an organism about its behavior can be considered a feedback mechanism. Simple feedback mechanisms are those that provide only one dimension of information to the organism regarding behavior occurring.

An example of a simple feedback mechanism would be a mechanical counter that simply recorded the number of problems completed in an arithmetic program. The student need only look at the counter to find out how many problems he had finished. Such a mechanism would give only information about the amount of a certain behavior occurring.

A more common feedback device which can be easily constructed by teacher and student alike is the histograph or cumulative graph. Students completing this particular unit when it was in the developmental process maintained graphs which gave feedback about a variety of academic and nonacademic behaviors. A sample of such behaviors are listed below:

Academic Behaviors:

Number of pages read/15 minutes

Number of words written/15 minutes

Number of minutes study/day
Number of trips to library/day
Percent of classes attended/day
Number of questions asked in class/class

Nonacademic Behaviors:

Number of Cokes consumed/day
Number of meals missed/day
Number of minutes spent on phone/day
Number of miles driven/day
Number of minutes with girl or boy friend/day

In Figure 8.1 a student used a graphic feedback mechanism to illustrate the percent of classes missed per school day. If the graph was maintained daily (and it was supposed to be), then the student could see from day to day how his behavior compared with other days and how close he was to his goal.

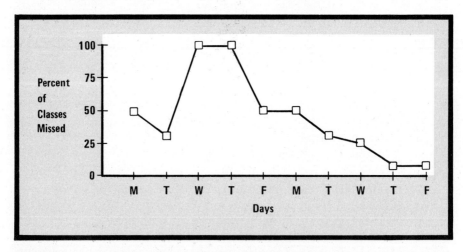

Figure 8.1 A graphic feedback mechanism (maintained by a student) showing percent of classes missed per day over a two week period.

Another graphic feedback mechanism is shown in Figure 8.2. In that case, the student wished to increase the number of pages he could read per fifteen minutes of reading. The steady progress was as obvious to him as it is to you looking at it now.

Graphs such as those in Figures 8.1 and 8.2 are often not meaningful to primary school children; so a more visually obvious device is needed. A bar

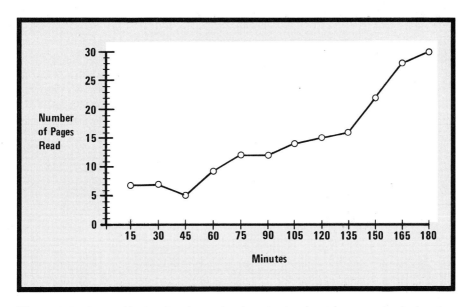

Figure 8.2 A graphic feedback mechanism (maintained by a student) showing number of pages read in Psychology text in 15 minute periods.

graph often provides the necessary graphic comparison. The tactic of using stars on some form of chart will also serve as a feedback mechanism, as long as the stars function as a means of providing information about progress instead of being token reinforcers themselves. In either case a change in behavior will be noted, but probably for different reasons. It is the author's opinion that the average elementary teacher is reasonably creative, and from that creativity will come a variety of ingenious feedback mechanisms that are suited to particular situations. In the past these have ranged from moving beads on an abacus to coloring in squares on a progress chart.

How do simple feedback mechanisms differ from more "complex" mechanisms?

Quantity of responses occurring need not be the only variable considered in feedback mechanisms. Quality could just as easily have been built into the graphs discussed earlier if it had been possible for the student to make correct and incorrect responses within the same behavior classification. For example, one could graph the number of arithmetic problems completed by a fourth grader, or the graph could just as easily show the number of arithmetic problems done *correctly*. These added conditions and the display of more information by the feedback mechanism make it more complex.

Consider two examples of complex feedback mechanisms: Imagine a situation where a mechanical device provides the correct answer to a problem for a student as soon as he states an answer. By comparing the display answer to his answer he can get information about the correctness of his behavior. With the addition of a counting device he could determine how many answers he had made to that point, and with a "correct answer" counting device he could determine how many correct answers he had made to that point.

A second illustration of a complex feedback mechanism is one used to train teachers such as interaction analysis which was explained in Unit Six. It is a technique used to provide information about several events occurring in a classroom. Interaction analysis data provide the following types of information:

1. The type of behavior occurring during any three second interval
2. The amount of a certain type of behavior occurring
3. The sequence of occurrence of various behaviors

Such a multiplicity of feedback from one mechanism makes it a complex device as opposed to the previously mentioned simple mechanisms.

What part does the "behavioral goal" play in feedback mechanisms?

In all the previous examples of feedback mechanisms, goals were implicitly present. Look for example at Figure 8.1. It is implicitly indicated that the goal for that student is to *reduce* the number of classes missed per day. It is not imprudent to go even a step further and assume that the absolute goal is "zero classes missed per day."

A goal, either implicit or explicit, must be part of every feedback mechanism in order for it to be optimally effective as a behavior change device. If the person receiving the feedback "doesn't care" how much or what behaviors he performs, then what difference does it make if the graph or other device indicates a rise or decline? It is for this reason that goals should be an integral part of feedback mechanisms. The way to insure their existence is to make them explicit. The person for whom the feedback mechanism is designed should be encouraged to set a specific goal.

What is meant by the relationship between setting goals and criterion performance?

The employment of a goal setting procedure in any educational endeavor has several functions. First, a well-constructed goal dictates the nature of the criterion performance. This aspect of education curricula is usually handled by using standardized achievement tests. However, the feedback to the student from a standardized test score is questionable. A grade-level score has very little significance to a student who has never discriminated the difference between the abilities displayed by the average third grader and the average fourth grader. To the fourth grade child with a reading deficiency, a pretest score of 2.5 and a post-test score of 2.7 means that, "I am two points better," and after a little thought, "And I read like a second grader, however that is . . ."

Most of us at some time or another have had the experience of being told that we, "write like an author," "play golf like a professional," or some similar comparison to an exalted standard of performance. Our first reaction is usually, "Oh," the second will probably be, "I wonder what I did that he does that makes him what he is?" At this point the student referred to above would be forced to look at a second grader and say to himself, "Whatever he's doing, I'm doing it, too." This can hardly be construed as valuable feedback.

How do goals function as "quality control measures"?

To the teacher, the goal which the student selects becomes a quality control measure of the education program. The behavior which the student wishes to incorporate into his repertoire can be set forth in exacting specifications. The teacher has adequately fulfilled his function when those specifications are met. The teacher who refuses to regard the goal of the student as a specification of instructional performance has made no more of a commitment to success than the student who refuses to set a goal.

To the student the establishment of a goal has value in that it provides a checkpoint where success is a reality. The concept of a commitment to success is important for both teacher and student alike. The poor student is viewed as a "system failure." The classroom as an instructional system is responsible for the construction and operation of a teaching environment which will maximize student success in accordance with specified goals and permit independent academic achievement. If the reading teacher cannot put his finger on the reading material which corresponds to the student's concept of reading, he cannot show the student that he has learned to read. The student, then, has a built-in failure factor. This factor provides security for the student who has been an academic failure and has learned to live with the image of a loser. Committing oneself to a reasonable, measurable goal is committing oneself to a chance for success. Committing oneself to an open-ended goal is tantamount to no commitment at all.

A definite goal (when reached) becomes an example of success as well as a foundation for further goals. The closer the goal, temporally, the greater the chance for success. The contract policy[3] operating in experimental class-rooms for children is an example of the establishment of short-term goals which can be reached in one hour or less if the student so desires.

How is goal setting related to motivation?

The last important aspect of goal setting is perhaps the most beneficial to the student. Since the goal is directed toward some area of pronounced information need, the student has indicated what topic areas are of interest to him and what type of information will keep him motivated. The teacher must then engineer the learning experience, building and developing the student's knowledge to the specifications set by the student. The materials needed for each student are those which contain the information necessary to attain his goal. Through the application of this methodology, classroom teachers can perform what might be their proper function; to provide students with those tools which are necessary in the acquisition and production of information.

The emphasis here must be placed on the word, "tools." Reading, for example, like arithmetic, is not an end in itself, but rather a means to an end. When the end is specified, and when attempts are made to use the tool which is the means to that end, every attempt which is to some degree successful will be an approach to that end, and, therefore, will be reinforcing. The beginning reader is learning to use a tool for gaining information. If the information to be gained by the student is specified and necessary, then any attempt at reading will also be an attempt to acquire that information. A successful reading experience automatically becomes a successful information processing experience.

How can goals be used for establishing a curriculum?

Depending on the entering skills of the student and the nature of the student goal, some goals can be achieved in a much shorter period of time than others. For instance, an adult reading at a 3.2 grade level will learn to read 5.0 grade-level workbooks in home economics sooner than will an adult reading at a 1.0 grade level. Or it would take a high-school sophomore reading at a 2.8 grade level longer to earn a high-school diploma than it would take for an adult with the same reading level to learn to read machine operating manuals.

3. L. Homme, et al, *How to Use Contingency Contracting in the Classroom* (Champaign, Ill.: Research Press, 1969).

Which student below is likely to achieve his goal sooner?

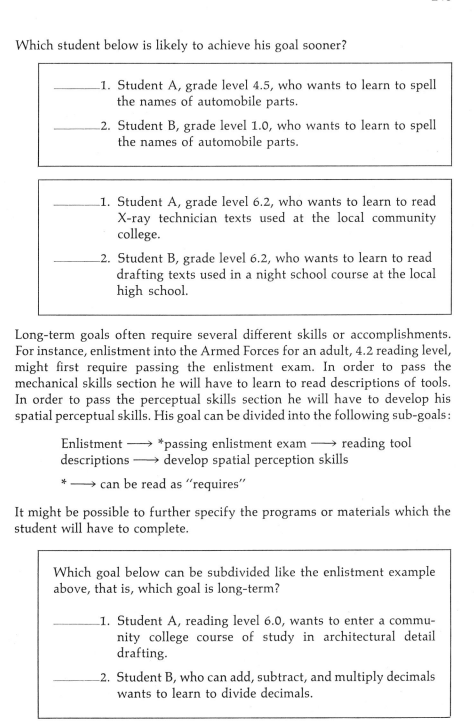

> _____1. Student A, grade level 4.5, who wants to learn to spell the names of automobile parts.
>
> _____2. Student B, grade level 1.0, who wants to learn to spell the names of automobile parts.

> _____1. Student A, grade level 6.2, who wants to learn to read X-ray technician texts used at the local community college.
>
> _____2. Student B, grade level 6.2, who wants to learn to read drafting texts used in a night school course at the local high school.

Long-term goals often require several different skills or accomplishments. For instance, enlistment into the Armed Forces for an adult, 4.2 reading level, might first require passing the enlistment exam. In order to pass the mechanical skills section he will have to learn to read descriptions of tools. In order to pass the perceptual skills section he will have to develop his spatial perceptual skills. His goal can be divided into the following sub-goals:

Enlistment $\longrightarrow$ *passing enlistment exam $\longrightarrow$ reading tool descriptions $\longrightarrow$ develop spatial perception skills

* $\longrightarrow$ can be read as "requires"

It might be possible to further specify the programs or materials which the student will have to complete.

> Which goal below can be subdivided like the enlistment example above, that is, which goal is long-term?
>
> _____1. Student A, reading level 6.0, wants to enter a community college course of study in architectural detail drafting.
>
> _____2. Student B, who can add, subtract, and multiply decimals wants to learn to divide decimals.

The subdividing of a goal, whether short or long-term, provides a course of study or curriculum for the student. The subdivisions become short-term goals or checkpoints on the path to the final goal. The course for the hypothetical student above would look like this:

Total-Task Chart For Student A

Word attack program ☐

Beginning Mechanics Book ☐

Advanced Tools Book ☐

Sample Mechanics Exam ☐

Elementary Spatial Problems ☐

Advanced Spatial Problems ☐

Sample Spatial Perception Exam ☐

Enlistment Exam ☐

Enlistment in Army ☐

Which example below can serve as a student course of study?

———1.   ———2.

Survey of local street names

Spelling exam pretest (first section)   Student: male, 10 years

Spelling program (first section)   of age

Spelling exam (first section)   Goal: to learn about

Spelling exam pretest (second section)   astronomy

Spelling program (second section)   Past Achievement: average

Spelling exam (second section)   Present reading grade

Spelling exam—city street names   level: 4.3

How can a total-task chart provide progress feedback?

A total-task chart can do more than just show the student his course of study. It can be used to:

1. provide a graphic record of progress toward the final goal;
2. provide a measure of partial success each time a sub-goal is reached.

For example, Jim's chart looked like this:

Book A	☒
Book B	☒
Book D	☒
Book I	☒
Book II	☒
Book I	☒
Book 2	☐
Book 3	☐
Book 4	☐
Book 5	☐
Word Skills Book	☐
Visual Tracking Book	☐
PROGRAM COMPLETION	☐

---

1. PROGRAM COMPLETION is a goal. Is Jim approximately:

_____a) half finished   OR,   _____b) a quarter finished

---

2. Tom has six workbooks which he has completed. He is working on a different task from Jim. He does not have a Total Task Chart. Without knowing the total number of books to complete his goal, can Tom say that he is one-half finished with that goal: _____Yes _____No

---

How can feedback mechanisms provide daily progress information?

In the previous question we established a means for providing information to a student about his progress toward a goal. It was assumed that without feedback a student might not be able to see his progress, and, therefore, not be able to recognize success. A graphic presentation such as a total-task chart allows the student to monitor rather large sequences of learning behavior, that is, he can see progress each time he completes a book or exercise.

Some students, however, need information about day to day performance. Charles, for instance, began to do less work at each session shortly after coming to school. It was predicted that he would soon quit—even before he had reached the first sub-goal of a larger final goal. The graph below was set up for him.

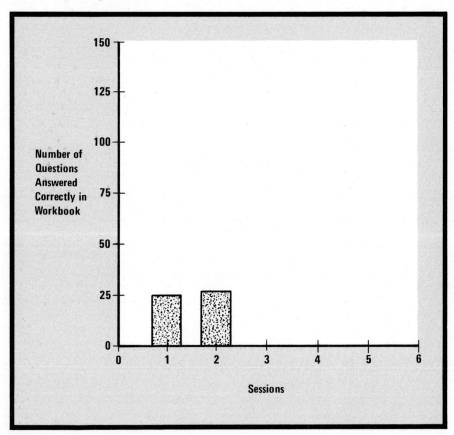

Figure 8.3 Feedback graph established for Charles to show performance levels from day-to-day.

Here is Charles's work output for each day in terms of questions answered: Session (1) 25, (2) 25, (3) 50, (4) 100, (5) 75, (6) 100. Complete the graph in Figure 8.3.

Here is a daily progress graph for an adult who is reading a radio repair book.

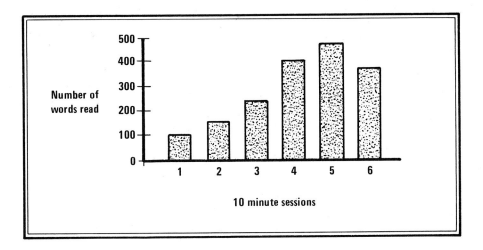

Complete the graph below for a student solving arithmetic problems in an elmentary business arithmetic program.

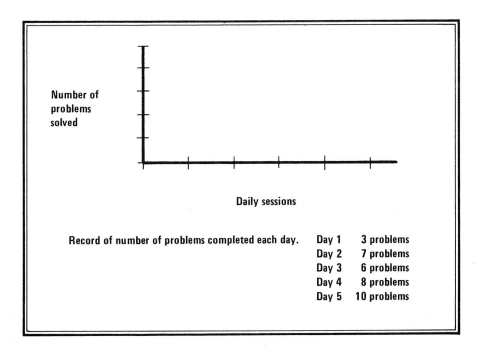

Number of problems solved

Daily sessions

Record of number of problems completed each day.	Day 1	3 problems
	Day 2	7 problems
	Day 3	6 problems
	Day 4	8 problems
	Day 5	10 problems

Which of the examples below gives the student the most information about his daily progress?

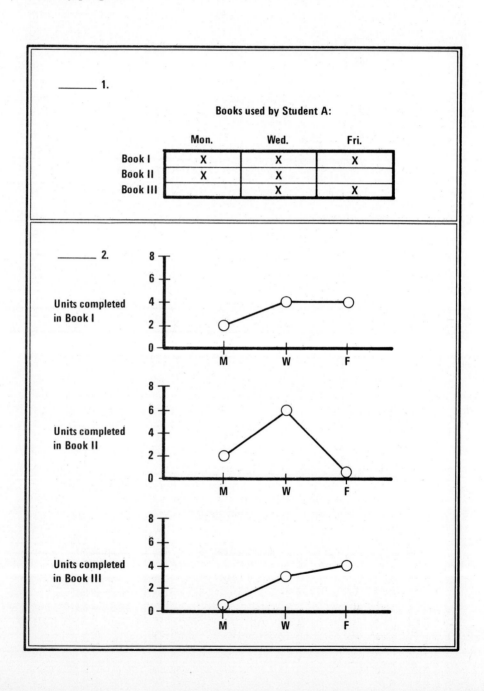

_____ 1.

Books used by Student A:

	Mon.	Wed.	Fri.
Book I	X	X	X
Book II	X	X	
Book III		X	X

_____ 2.

Units completed in Book I

Units completed in Book II

Units completed in Book III

♦ AN EXPERIENCE

The information on the previous pages is sufficient background to allow you to construct a feedback mechanism and experience the application of such a device. The experience aspect of this unit is described in the objectives below:

Experience Objectives

1. You should construct and maintain two (2) feedback mechanisms for modifying your behavior. One mechanism should be designed to modify study-related behavior; the other should involve nonacademic behavior. If you are not a student, you can still modify such study-related behaviors as writing, reading, studying a particular topic of your interest, etc.
2. You should help another person define a goal, construct and maintain a feedback mechanism.
3. You should prepare a report of the progress achieved with the mechanisms.

Suggested Procedure for Achieving the Experience Objectives

1. Make certain you have read the Background material and can answer all the questions.
2. Select a study-related and a nonacademic behavior you wish to modify. Complete the Study-Related Behavior Feedback Mechanism Assignment Sheet and the Nonacademic Behavior Feedback Mechanism Assignment Sheet.
3. Set up your feedback mechanism and maintain it for at least 7 days.
4. Locate someone who will agree to work toward the modification of a particular behavior. Help that person identify the behavior and construct a feedback mechanism. Arrange to have the person maintain that mechanism.
5. Complete Feedback Mechanism for Another Person Assignment Sheet.
6. Prepare a report of the progress. (If graphs were the major feedback device, label clearly the unit of behaviors measured and the interval of measurement used. If graphs were not the major feedback device, you should submit a short description of the feedback mechanism and some objective record of behavior change.)

Progress Chart

	Activity	Check each space when completed.
1.	Read Background	_____
2.	Study-related behavior selected	_____
3.	Nonacademic behavior selected	_____
4.	Study-Related Behavior Feedback Mechanism Assignment Sheet complete	_____
5.	Nonacademic Behavior Feedback Mechanism Assignment Sheet complete	_____
6.	Study-related feedback mechanism maintained for 7 days minimum	_____
7.	Nonacademic feedback mechanism maintained for 7 days minimum	_____
8.	Feedback mechanism prepared for another person	_____
9.	Feedback Mechanism for Another Person: Assignment Sheet complete	_____
10.	Progress Report complete	_____

Study-Related Behavior Feedback Mechanism

ASSIGNMENT SHEET

1. You are to construct and maintain a feedback mechanism for modifying nonacademic behavior. Describe the behavior you wish to modify.

2. What is the goal of the modification? What level of responding are you striving for?

3. What is the estimated frequency of responding now (X times/hr., Y times/day)?

4. Do you expect some secondary effect from this modification? (Such as more money, more free time, better grade.)

5. What is the feedback interval?

6. Describe the feedback mechanism or include it with this sheet.

Nonacademic Behavior Feedback Mechanism
ASSIGNMENT SHEET

1. You are to construct and maintain a feedback mechanism for modifying nonacademic behavior. Describe the behavior you wish to modify.

2. What is the goal of the modification? What level of responding are you striving for?

3. What is the frequency of responding now?

4. Do you expect some secondary effect from this modification?

5. What is the feedback interval?

6. Describe the feedback mechanism or include it with this sheet.

Feedback Mechanism For Another Person
ASSIGNMENT SHEET

1. You are to help another student define an academic goal and construct and maintain a feedback mechanism. What behavior will that person be modifying?

2. What is your relationship to that person? What influence might that relationship have on the results?

3. What is the goal of the modification?

4. What is the estimated frequency of responding now?

5. What secondary effect does the person expect from this modification?

6. What is the feedback interval?

7. Describe the feedback mechanism or include it with this sheet.

♦ SUMMARY

The particular approach described in this unit can be viewed as a product of the technological age. Many of the machines and devices which have accompanied the technological revolution have been used to send, receive, or store information. Since human beings perform many of the same tasks, the analyses necessary to produce effective machines have offered a new and exciting way of looking at man. The particular approach discussed in this unit has been called information theory. The background aspect of this unit dealt with one segment of information theory, feedback.

Feedback was defined as information coming to a control center which can be used to alter subsequent behavior. Three variables were identified which influence the functioning of feedback mechanisms: the feedback interval, the specificity of the information, and the goal of the organism or machine. The relationships between feedback devices and human behavior were pointed out. The use of feedback in an educational setting was described along with several other examples of the use of feedback to modify academic and nonacademic behaviors.

The experience portion suggested the use of simple feedback devices to modify an academic and nonacademic behavior of the reader. By building and maintaining such devices, it was hoped that the reader would be better prepared to critically evaluate the potential of this approach for solving teaching and learning problems. Since most teachers would be required to construct feedback mechanisms for their students, it was recommended that the reader find someone who would agree to identify and attempt to modify an academic behavior through the use of feedback. After constructing, maintaining, and evaluating three different feedback mechanisms for three different behaviors, the reader should be prepared to consider a number of questions about the utilization of information theory and feedback in the classroom.

Probably the foremost question to consider in relation to this unit is, Did the feedback mechanism work? Or more specifically, Did the person's behavior change sufficiently to reach the goal as stated? If not, Did it begin to change? Can a trend be identified? Feedback mechanisms are not foolproof devices. They are not automatic panaceas for man's behavior problems. However, it is possible to identify some of the reasons why they don't function as one would hope. A common shortcoming in many feedback mechanisms is the use of overly lengthy feedback intervals. For instance, the interval of one hour in a feedback device which shows the number of pages read per hour might be too long. Measuring the number of pages read per fifteen minutes might provide feedback which has a more immediate effect on the alteration of subsequent behavior.

Another shortcoming that is often seen is the use of a mechanism which does not sufficiently illustrate the level of performance or the change in performance from one interval to another. A simple illustration of this is the case where a line graph is employed, but the subject just places a dot at the level of performance for a certain interval and never connects succeeding dots by a line. Try it sometime: draw a graph and enter data which indicates a subtle trend but do not draw lines between the points. The connecting lines give the person using the graph a visual projection of the slope of performance levels. Could you see either of the two mentioned problems in the feedback mechanism with which you worked? It is certainly advisable for you to consider an engineering approach to the construction and maintainance of feedback mechanisms. That is, if the device you initially develop doesn't function adequately, then identify its weak points, rebuild it, and test its efficiency after modifications.

A further question you might consider at this time is, Whether or not the feedback mechanism worked, do I want to use such constricting devices on human beings? This question is basically philosophical in nature. The position could be taken that man should not aspire to a highly organized, controlled, and regulated existence. Adequate defense could be offered for the position that the richness of life is its diversity, its spontaneity, and its freedom from controls.

On the other hand, consider the notion that adequate feedback might help humans identify and more fully appreciate diversity, spontaneity, and freedom. One manner in which this could be accomplished is to provide feedback mechanisms for those activities which are required; those which man must do to maintain his chosen level of existence. Perhaps, those activities are the primary cause for anxiety, concern, or uncertainty. Reduce the uncertainty in those areas, and, maybe, the individual can achieve more freedom in the remaining areas.

Once again, we come back to the question which must be applied to each and every approach to learning and teaching, Do I wish to adopt this approach or some portion of it? In order to answer that question you might wish to have more information upon which to make a decision. If so, you might consider doing the Suggested Additional Activity and some of the Suggested Additional Readings for Unit Eight.

♦ A SUGGESTED ADDITIONAL ACTIVITY

It was suggested in the Background section of this unit that shorter feedback intervals provide more constant information, therefore also provide greater control over behavior. You could do an experiment which would test this principle. Use yourself as the subject (or if you have another person willing to participate, use that person). Select a novel which you have not previously read. Assume that you must for some reason read it in the shortest possible time. As a performance measure, count the number of *lines read* per feedback interval. Plan on two separate 30 minute periods during which you will read the novel. In period one set the feedback interval at five minutes. This means that during period one you will count the number of lines read each five minutes. During period two, count the number of lines read each ten minutes. Make certain that you separate periods one and two by at least an hour or two. Why?

After period two is complete, you should compare the data from the two periods. First, is the total number of pages read greater in one than the other? Is the difference great enough so that you can attribute it to the difference in feedback intervals? A small difference could occur by chance. Psychological researchers have statistical tests and tables to refer to in order to determine whether or not differences are *significant;* that is, they are not likely to occur by chance. A second bit of information you can look at from your data is the slope of the performance curve. Did you increase or decrease number of lines read from the first feedback interval to the last? Were there sharp differences between any two intervals? If marked differences did occur, can you offer reasons why this might have happened? Did the content of the novel change or influence your rate of reading at that point? Would a shorter feedback interval have been helpful at that point? Why?

It is not very common for a single variable like feedback interval to have absolute control over performance. That is, other variables like fatigue, content of subject matter, and reinforcement will have some influence on behavior. An exercise like the one described above will help you to identify other variables or, at least, recognize the influence of other variables besides the one you are controlling.

♦ SUGGESTED ADDITIONAL READINGS

For Basic Information on Feedback and Information Theory

Fitts, P. M., and Posner, M. I. *Human Performance.* Belmont, California: Brooks/ Cole, 1967.

Simon, H. A. *The Sciences of the Artificial.* Cambridge, Mass.: MIT Press, 1969.

For More Advanced Information

Bilodeau, E. A. *Supplementary Feedback and Instructions.* In E. A. Bilodeau ed. "Principles of Skill Acquisition." New York: Academic Press, 1969, 235–251.

Bilodeau, I. McD. *Information Feedback.* In E. A. Bilodeau ed. "Acquisition of Skill." New York: Academic Press, 1966, 255–282.

Haber, R. N. *Information Processing Approaches to Visual Perception.* New York: Holt, Rinehart and Winston, 1969.

Raisbeck, G. *Information Theory.* Cambridge, Mass.: MIT Press, 1963.

Wiener, N. *Cybernetics.* Cambridge, Mass.: MIT Press, 1948.

For Information Regarding Specific Application of Feedback

Amidon, E. J., and Flanders, N. A. "Interaction Analysis as a Feedback System." In E. J. Amidon and J. B. Hough eds. *Interaction Analysis: Theory, Research and Application.* Reading, Mass.: Addison-Wesley, 1967, 121–140.

Leitenberg, H.; Agras, W. S.; Thompson, L. E.; and Wright, D. E. "Feedback in Behavior Modification: an Experimental Analysis in Two Phobic Cases." *Journal of Applied Behavior Analysis* 1(1968):131–138.

Minsky, M. L. "Artificial Intelligence." *Scientific American* 215(1966):246–260.

Smode, A. F. "Learning and Performance in a Tracking Task Under Two Levels of Achievement Information Feedback." *Journal of Experimental Psychology* 56(1958):297–304.

Tuckman, B. W.; McCall, K. M.; and Hyman, R. T. "The Modification of Teacher Behavior: Effects of Dissonance and Coded Feedback." *American Educational Research Journal* 6(1969):501–515.

Tustin, A. "Feedback." *Scientific American* 187 (1962):48–55.

UNIT 9

Instructional Design

♦ BACKGROUND

The development of behavioristic theories of human learning has stimulated
a good bit of applied psychological research. A considerable amount of that
research deals with the factors involved in designing instructional sequences,
particularly those aspects which encompass the actual learning act. Psychologists concerned with this particular area often select as a dependent
variable the amount of information learned, the time required to learn the
information, or the amount of information retained over varying lengths of
time. Obviously, the approach of psychologists concerned with instructional
design is very closely related to what might be called an "applied learning
theory" approach.

Utilizing the combined instructional design and applied learning theory
approaches has led some psychologists to develop methods for programming
or "engineering" learning. Since the learning must be measured, it is always
in the form of some behavior acquisition. Therefore, what has been developed is a form of "behavior engineering." Educational psychologists
have suggested that teachers might find it valuable to act as behavioral
engineers. Like an engineer a teacher could specify the type of structure
(behavior) to be built and be capable of evaluating whether or not the
structure was built to specification. If it is the case that the behavior was not
successfully established, the teacher could revise the teaching methodology.
This is analogous to saying that the engineer builds a bridge differently the
second time if it doesn't stay up the first time.

Whether or not the teacher is or wishes to be a behavioral engineer, the
techniques associated with programming or designing instructional se-

quences often prove to be innovative and provide useful as well as exciting alternatives for the educator. In this unit the individual steps of instructional design will be dealt with as separate parts of a whole process. The purpose for this format is to enable the reader to select or reject those segments which appear to be useful or useless under particular circumstances. The experience will involve some practice with programming skills, but before actually practicing the various skills, some background information should be considered.

What are the basic components of the method used to engineer or program behavior?

There are several detailed steps to the complete method of programming instruction, but at this point let us consider only the general phases of the overall procedure. Five general phases which are often practiced are:

1. Specify the behavior to be learned.

   Example: In a preschool setting the teacher specifies that "The child will place knife and spoon on right side of dish and fork on left side when setting a table."

2. Develop a way of measuring whether or not the behavior in 1. above was learned.

   Example: For the above-mentioned preschool situation the teacher will ask the child to place four knives, forks and spoons in their correct positions at a table used by the children.

3. Develop an instructional procedure for teaching the behavior in 1 above.

   Example: The teacher in the preschool situation decided to let older children in the primary grades teach the preschoolers in a mock-up "restaurant" established by the primary-grade children.

4. Implement the instructional procedure and measurement in 2 and 3 above.

   Example: The preschoolers were given the test of placing the four sets of dinnerware in the correct positions before going to the primary grade "restaurant" for instruction. The children who could already correctly position the dinnerware *did not* go for instruction, while the others who could not do it correctly did receive instruction from the primary-grade children for two consecutive days. Upon returning to the preschool classroom, the children receiving instruction were tested again using the same measurement as previously.

5. Revise the instructional procedure if the measurement instrument indicates the behavior was not learned.

Example: About 40 percent of the children (preschoolers) could not consistently place the fork and spoon in the correct position. The teacher for the preschool children discovered that these children had been given instruction by the boys in the primary grade "restaurant," and the rest of the preschoolers had received instruction from the girls and learned the desired behavior. The instructional strategy was revised so that the primary-grade girls only gave instructions on table setting, while the boys were used for other projects.

From the five general phases and examples described above, it can be seen that "programming" instruction does not always result in a stereotyped, paper-and-pencil style of programmed instruction. For many years the only instructional sequences produced which were programmed were the fill-in-the-blanks workbook type. In such a program the student would write in the answer to a question after being given the information just moments earlier. Such programs led to accusations from teachers that programs were intellectually insulting, boring, and just plain useless. Whether the accusations are true or not is irrelevant to this unit. What is relevant is the notion that programmed instruction need not be limited to a single style of instructional presentation, and the important aspect of instructional design is the preparatory methodology. Let us now look more closely at that methodology.

What is the first thing one does when preparing an instructional sequence?

The first general phase stated previously was "Specify the behavior to be learned." There are two specific steps within that general phase, the behavior or task analysis step and the statement of objectives step. Figure 9.1 illustrates this part of the methodology.

The behavior or task analysis step is probably the most critical aspect of the whole methodology. This is the time when the teacher analyzes exactly what the student will learn to do, and exactly how it is done. Note the emphasis on the words, "do," "behavior," "response," and "task" rather than on more commonly used words like "know," "understand," or "appreciate." The reason for this emphasis rests with the need for the teacher to be able to measure what has been learned without making unwarranted inferences. For example, suppose a teacher said, "I want my students to *understand* the causes of the Civil War." Now, that sounds like a reasonable general objective, and probably no one would take undue issue with it, but the question does arise, How will you check to see if they *understand*? Our imaginary teacher might say, "Well, I would test them." The next question to the teacher has to be, How will you test them? The teacher replies, "I'll

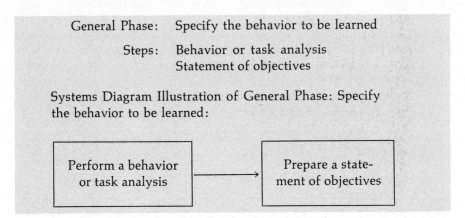

General Phase: Specify the behavior to be learned

Steps: Behavior or task analysis
Statement of objectives

Systems Diagram Illustration of General Phase: Specify the behavior to be learned:

Perform a behavior or task analysis → Prepare a statement of objectives

Figure 9.1   Explanation of the General Phase: Specify the behavior to be learned, of the methodology for programming instruction.

give them an essay question like, *List and elaborate on the causes of the Civil War.*" Now, we must ask the question, If a student can answer that question correctly, you will be satisfied that he *understands* the causes of the Civil War? If the teacher responds, "Yes," then, the task or behavior that you want the child to perform is *"to write a list of the causes of the Civil War and elaborate on the items in the list."* This last statement is a description of the behavior the teacher wants the student to perform in order to infer that some "understanding" of the subject matter has been achieved. The teacher is not through yet, however, because the behavior of ". . . elaborate on the items in the list" must be broken down. What behaviors does a student perform when he "elaborates"? Let us assume that for the teacher in question there are two specific components within the elaboration of a statement: one is to define the terms in the statement; the other is to give examples.

The imaginary teacher we have been working with has now completed the first two steps of the programming methodology. The behavior the student is to learn has been analyzed, and the statement of objectives for the student has been made; i.e., *the student will write a list of the causes of the Civil War and elaborate on the items on the list by defining the terms and giving examples.*

Unlike the example just given, analyzing the behavior which the student will eventually perform is often an extremely difficult job. The strategies for completing an analysis are varied, and few, if any, have been shown to be thoroughly valid. The following example is another approach to the task or behavior analysis step, and it is commonly known as "flow charting." Flow charting works particularly well when the analyst has direct observation of the master performer; that is, when the person doing the task analysis can watch someone who already is proficient in doing the task. Almost all behavior chains performed by humans can be fitted to a flow chart.

In its simplest form, flow charting consists of the use of "action boxes or rectangles" and "decision diamonds"; i.e., boxes or rectangles are used to graphically represent actions while diamonds are used to represent decision points. In addition, it is often desirable to state assumptions regarding the organism and its environment. This saves the teacher from having to follow out all the "exceptions" or "subsystems" arising during the analysis.

For example, the flow chart in Figure 9.2 illustrates how the major aspects of a behavior chain can be specified in flow-chart form.

The following assumptions were stated for the intramuscular injection flow chart:

1. The proper equipment is present, a sterile hypodermic syringe and needle, proper medication, alcohol swabs.
2. The physician has ordered the medication for a particular patient.
3. It is proper time for injection.
4. Medication has been properly prepared in the syringe.

It is obvious that the task to be learned in the example above is related to the nursing profession and would probably be taught in a nursing education program. The flow chart handles the task analysis step, and the statement of objectives step can be completed with the aid of the flow chart. For example the first action to be performed during this particular task is to "ask the patient his name." That is a skill which most student nurses will have; so the teacher need not state the objective "the student will ask the patient for his name." However, the next part of the flow chart which is a decision box might require some instruction and, hence, an objective. The decision to be made is, Is the name on the medication ticket the same as the patient gave you? Because of similarities in surnames and given names the student nurse will have to learn to look for an *exact* match between the name on the ticket and the name given by the patient. The teacher might state the following objective for that decision, "Given a situation in which a medication ticket is available and a patient recites his name, the student will state whether or not the medication is to be given to that patient." By progressing from stage to stage on the flow chart, the teacher can decide what should be learned and generate objectives for that behavior.

Another method of doing a task or behavior analysis was developed by Robert Glaser[1] and has been called the Ruleg system. Basically, the Ruleg

1. R. Glaser, "The Ruleg System for Construction of Programmed Verbal Learning Sequences." In R. Glaser ed., *Investigation of the Characteristics of Programmed Learning Sequences* (Pittsburgh: University of Pittsburgh, 1961), pp. 17–30.

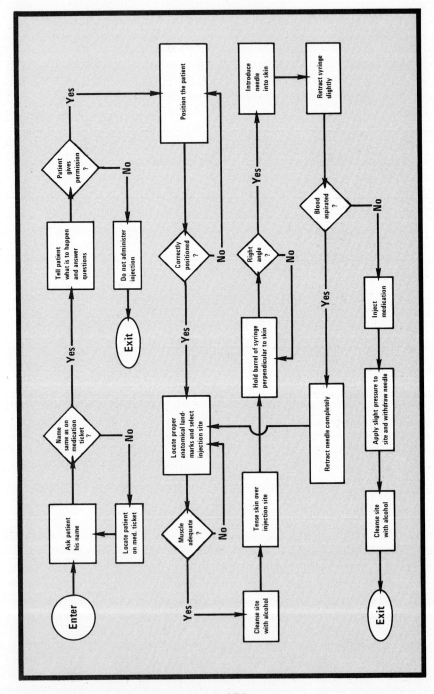

Figure 9.2 Flow-chart analysis: The administration of an intramuscular injection to a patient.

270

system is an analysis method in which the teacher states the rules (rul's) which can be applied to a specific behavior and generates examples (eg's) of those rules. Teaching usually involves the presentation of combinations of rules and examples.

During the initial analysis, rules are ordered according to temporal sequence; i.e., those which must come earlier in a behavior chain precede those which come later in a chain. Rules are, also, ordered according to dependence; i.e., if a behavior cannot be performed unless some other behavior has already occurred, then the one behavior is dependent upon the other and must follow it in order. The teacher must consider the possibility of combining certain rules or defining overlapping rules.

Examples are generated according to the criteria of sufficiency and frequency. Enough examples must be generated for each rule to insure that the range of possible appropriate behaviors is represented. Those examples occurring most frequently in the real-life situation are important to consider.

To illustrate the Ruleg analysis technique let us look at the intramuscular injection flow chart again. Here is a Rul and an Eg which could be stated from that task:

Rul: The name which the patient gives you must be identical to that on the medication ticket.

Eg: Nurse X would not give Z medication to Mr. R. T. Smith because the name on Z medication was R. Smith.

The rest of the parts of the total act of giving an intramuscular injection can be analyzed in a manner similar to the Rul and Eg stated above, that is, Ruls and Egs can be stated for each of the discrete acts within the total behavior chain. From the list of Ruls and Egs, the teacher can develop a set of objectives appropriate to the task.

Just a note about stating objectives: there are several good books on the technique of wording objectives; so the reader will not be given practice with that skill in this book. (See the Suggested Additional Readings for this unit for specific book titles.) The reader should note, however, from the examples of objectives given, that objectives must be measurable and stated in terms of student behavior. The latter point is a subtle one. Most teachers are accustomed to stating objectives in terms of what teachers do. For example, "I will expose my students to the various farm animals by taking them to a farm," is fairly typical of educational objectives. Such a statement is incorrect *according to programming methodology* because it is not stated in terms of student behavior but rather teacher behavior.

To summarize several points made in answer to the question, What is the first thing one does when programming an instructional sequence?

A. Under the general phase, "Specify the behavior to be learned" are two steps:
1. a behavior or task analysis
2. a statement of objectives.

B. The task or behavior analysis is the most important part of the programming methodology.

C. Flow charting and Ruleg analysis methods are two ways of doing an analysis.

D. Objectives should be stated in terms of student behavior and the behavior described should be measurable.

Describe the second general phase of programming instruction.

The second general phase of programming instruction was, "Develop a way of measuring whether or not the behavior in 1 above was learned." The "1 above" refers to the first general phase, "Specify the behavior to be learned." The method most often used for measuring the learning of a student is the paper and pencil test. Most students are quite familiar with essay, multiple choice, true and false, and completion tests by the time they reach the secondary grades. Unfortunately, few teachers have moved away from the "written test" as a means of evaluating student progress. In the programming methodology, however, the written test is used only when it is the most appropriate means of measuring whether or not the objective has been met. Remember the earlier example of the preschool children learning to set tables? Which is the more appropriate measure of the teacher's objectives in that case? Would it be a table with actual dinnerware to be set; or a question like, Which side, right or left, does the fork go on? If you have trouble making the choice, think about the task of saying "right" or "left" given the stimulus cue, "fork" or "knife," as opposed to the motor behavior of placing the fork in the correct place even without being able to name it as the right or left. Of course, the answer to the question regarding which is the more appropriate measure is that the actual behavior the teacher desires is the one which should be measured, hence, the student should put actual dinnerware at a table.

A special bit of terminology has been developed to refer to the test which measures the behavior the teacher desires. It is often called the "criterion measure," because it is the last or ultimate behavior which is to be engineered. The behavior in the criterion measure must be identical to the behavior described in the objective.

The important point a teacher should keep in mind when preparing a way of measuring whether or not the student has learned the behavior specified in the objectives is that the teacher must be satisfied that the objective has been met if the student performs correctly on the criterion measure. If the student gets a "perfect" score on the criterion measurement instrument, and the teacher is not satisfied that the objective has been met, then the criterion measurement is inadequate.

Describe the general phase in which the instructional procedure is developed.

It is important to point out that in spite of having selected and analyzed a behavior as well as preparing a criterion measure, the teacher has not yet considered the problem of how to teach the behavior. This is an important point and, perhaps represents the hardest adjustment for teachers to make. (The author considers it an adjustment because most educators tend to be "methodologically prone"; that is, the method controls all other aspects of the learning and teaching process including the objectives and outcome. Very few teachers stop to ask themselves, Where do I want to go with my students? before considering, How am I going to get there?)

If the teacher waits to consider the actual instructional procedure until after the analysis, objectives, and criterion measurement instruments have been produced, then he can enjoy the luxury of selecting the procedure which will best do the job. He will not be tied to a particular procedure, nor will he have to argue for his choice of procedures. All he need do if questioned is point to the objectives and say, "This instructional procedure in my opinion is the one which will best reach those objectives, and after I have tried it, I will have evidence to support or deny my opinions."

Developing an instructional procedure necessitates knowing something about human learning. It means for example that the teacher must decide how much material to present, and in what order, and whether the material should be visual, aural, or tactual, or even a combination of the three. The procedure finally selected must be constrained by the characteristics of the students involved. It must be practical within the educational setting for which it is designed as well as within the budget of the teacher involved. It is obvious that a single, all-purpose procedure for teaching a behavior or skill has not yet been identified, nor is it ever likely to be. There are, however, a couple of general principles a teacher can follow when developing an instructional procedure to meet a criterion measurement instrument and set of objectives previously developed.

PRINCIPLE 1

In any instructional sequence the student *must be called upon to* make regularly scheduled responses relating to the task to be learned.

EXAMPLE

If Billy is learning to print his name, he must make a series of responses which lead to and which approximate the final task of printing, "Billy." Depending on his beginning level, he might start by printing a "B," then an "i," then a "Bi," etc.

PRINCIPLE 2

Before being called upon to "produce" the correct response for a given task, the student must be called upon to "identify" the correct response.

COROLLARY 2–1

The difference between a "production" and an "identification" response is that in the former the student recalls or generates the response from memory, whereas in the latter the student chooses the correct response from given alternatives.

COROLLARY 2–2

If the criterion measure involves only an identification response, then the student need only make identification responses during instruction.

EXAMPLE

Billy's criterion measure is to print his name. Before being called upon to print "B," he should be given the task of identifying (pointing to or circling) the "B" when it is paired with such other letters as the "I," "E," "F," etc.

PRINCIPLE 3

In any *instructional sequence,* that is, any sequence of responses where the student is supposed to learn something, a model or example of the response he is to identify or produce should be available.

COROLLARY 3–1

In any *testing sequence* the model should not be available.

COROLLARY 3–2

Examples are concrete instances of a generalized statement.

EXAMPLE

Billy is still learning to print his name. If the first response called for is to identify the "B" when given the "B" and "P" together, he should also have a model of the "B" available.

Teacher says, "This is the 1st letter in your name."

"Circle the one down here which is like the one above."

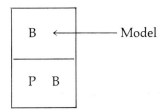

OBSERVATION 1

Visual models are currently easier than auditory models to make constantly available. Imagine the difficulty encountered in a "bird call" program in which a response called for is to identify the Cardinal call when given two bird calls. How do you keep the model, a Cardinal call, available? You could say to the student, "Here is a Cardinal call," and present the proper call. Then say, "Which of these two is a Cardinal call?" The student in that sequence must keep the model call in memory or be allowed to ask for a repetition of the model whenever necessary.

PRINCIPLE 4

If the behavior to be learned calls for deductive or inductive responses (as opposed to rote recitation), then learning will be enhanced by the addition of examples to the instructional procedure.

PRINCIPLE 5

In any instructional sequence where an identification response is called for, the number of alternatives should be two.

COROLLARY 5–1

In preparing an instructional sequence, the incorrect alternative of the pair given in an identification response task should initially be a choice which is least like the model and later as close to the model as necessary.

EXAMPLE

Billy still can't print his name because the teacher gave him a model for the "B" but asked him to identify the "B" when given the "P," "d," "E," and "H." The teacher should have made the model "B" available while asking Billy to choose the correct letter when given the "B" and the "M" and so forth—working eventually closer to those letters (P, d, E, H) which are like the "B."

Explain what is meant by "implementation and revision" of the instructional procedure.

"Implementing the instructional procedure" simply means that the teacher tries the material out on the students for whom it was designed. There are five steps to this general phase. The steps are described in Figure 9.3.

First, the teacher evaluates the extent of the student's behavior repertoire before instruction begins by giving him the test, that is, administering

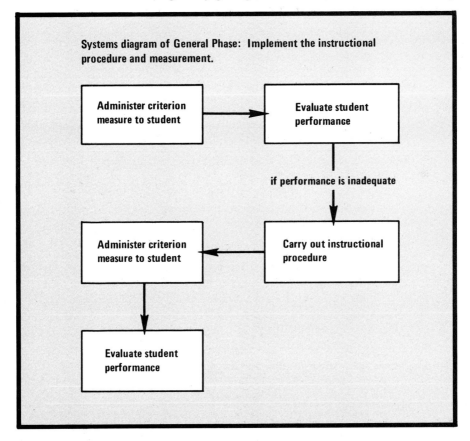

Figure 9.3 Explanation of General Phase: Implement the instructional procedure and measurement.

the criterion measure. Second, the teacher must determine whether or not the student's behavior is already adequate. Instruction is not necessary if the student can respond appropriately to the criterion measure. Third, for the students who cannot perform adequately on the criterion measure, the teacher carries out the instructional procedure as it was designed. Fourth, the criterion measure is given again after the instructional procedure is completed. Fifth, the student's responses on the criterion measure are evaluated again.

The final general phase of the programming methodology for instructional design was to "Revise the instructional procedure if the criterion measurement instrument indicates the behavior was not learned." The teacher has to decide whether or not the instructional procedure was adequate based on the student's performance. If they did not perform at the level desired after instruction, then the instructional procedure requires revision. The notion of revising the instructional procedure based on the performance data of the students is of utmost importance to instructional design. It is not unusual for most teachers to revise the *content* of the instruction, but given the amount of "lecturing" which goes on in classrooms across the country, it is probably unusual for a teacher to revise *instructional procedures* on the basis of student performance.

General Phase: Implement the instructional procedure and measurement.

Steps: Administer the criterion measure to the student.

Determine if student behavior is adequate before instruction.

Carry out instructional procedure.

Administer the criterion measure to the students receiving instruction.

Determine if student behavior is adequate after instruction.

Put all the General Phases and steps together to illustrate the complete programming procedure.

Below is an outline of the General Phases and steps within the phases:
General Phase 1: Specify the behavior to be learned.
Steps: Behavior or task analysis
Statement of objectives
General Phase 2: Develop a way of measuring whether or not the behavior in 1 above was learned.
General Phase 3: Develop an instructional procedure for teaching the behavior in 1 above.

General Phase 4: Implement the instructional procedure and measurement.
   Steps: Administer the criterion measure to the student.
      Determine if student behavior is adequate before instruction.
      Carry out instructional procedure.
      Administer the criterion measure to the students receiving instruction.
      Determine if student behavior is adequate after instruction.

General Phase 5: Revise the instructional procedure if the criterion measurement instrument indicates the behavior was not learned.

The systems diagram or flow chart in Figure 9.4 illustrates the actions and decisions involved in the complete programming procedure.

Give an example of how this method can be used by a teacher.

As an example of how the programming methodology can be used by a teacher, let us consider Mrs. Mitchell who is a senior high school physical education teacher. As a new behavior for her students in golf class, Mrs. Mitchell selected "knowing how to chip a golf ball onto a sloping green." "Knowing how" was not something the students might "do"; so she decided to select instead the behavior of "chipping onto a sloping green."

Mrs. Mitchell decided that she could best analyze this task by identifying the rules which apply and examples of those rules. She decided that there were only three rules which a beginning golfer needs when chipping onto a green. All three rules were stated like the one below.

Rule 1: If the ball is on the apron (just off the green), and the green slopes downhill from the right to the left, you must hit the ball to the right of the cup or uphill of it.

Examples were awkward to write; so Mrs. Mitchell drew some pictures to serve as examples of each rule.

Having completed the analysis step, Mrs. Mitchell began stating behavioral objectives. They looked like this:

The student will chip the ball from the apron to within 3 feet of the cup in a situation where the green slopes from right to left enough to influence the path of the ball.

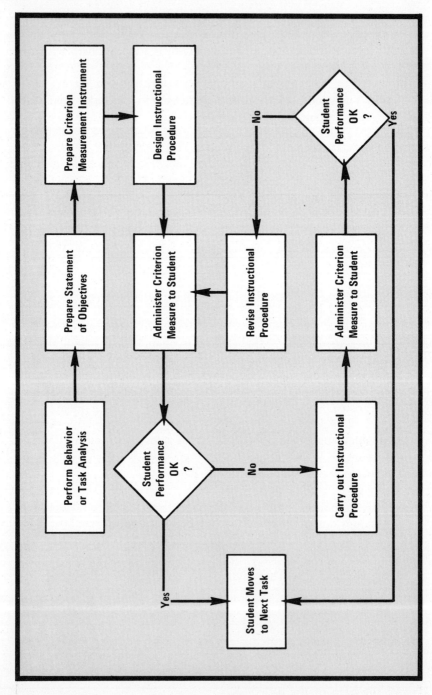

Figure 9.4 General Flow Chart for Instructional Programming Procedure.

Objectives were stated for all of the possible situations which were to be taught.

Luckily, the school in which Mrs. Mitchell taught had a practice green alongside the athletic fields. She placed small, white, numbered pegs in the ground at the points where students should place the ball when demonstrating their ability to perform the desired behavior. This was the criterion measure.

As an instructional procedure Mrs. Mitchell decided to simply give each student a sheet with the list of rules printed on it and give a lecture on the reasons why these rules were necessary.

Next, she administered the test which only one person passed. That one girl was allowed to work on hitting the ball off the tee which was something she didn't do well. Back in the gym after the test, the rest of the students were given the materials and presented with the explanation for the rules.

During the next period, the students were tested again, and Mrs. Mitchell found that very few could achieve the objectives. Casual observation told her that the students did not use the rules at first, but with practice, most could achieve the objectives as stated. She decided to revise the instructional procedure to delete the lecture and add a period of practice hits from locations around the green which were designated by blue pegs. Before taking practice rounds, the students were required to correctly identify pictures which were associated with each rule. When the revised instructional procedure was carried out with the next class of students, 90 percent achieved the objectives. Mrs. Mitchell was satisfied with these results and decided to provide further practice for the remaining 10 percent.

♦ AN EXPERIENCE

How is the experience aspect of this unit related to the programming procedure for instructional design?

The "design of the instructional procedure" and "implementation" phases are emphasized in the experience portion of this unit. Remember that by the time a teacher is ready for the implementation phase, a criterion measurement instrument is ready and so is an instructional procedure. Both of these things have been prepared in advance for you so that you can carry out the instructional procedure with a subject. The instructional procedure has been designed in two different ways so that you can observe the influence on learning when examples are systematically included in instruction. The first set of instructional materials is the "first draft version" and does not include examples; while the second set of materials is the "revised draft version" and does include examples. As you give the programs to various subjects, it is hoped that you will see the "power" of examples, and their positive influence on the instructional procedure.

The programs were designed to be used as a supplement to a regular course; that is, the purpose of the program is to provide a means by which the student can teach himself the "Dynamic Transpositional Interaction Technique."

The Experience Objectives will help to clarify exactly what you are to do.

Experience Objectives

1. You should arrange to have four subjects complete the Dynamic Transpositional Interaction Theory I program, and four other subjects complete the Dynamic Transpositional Interaction Theory II program.
2. You should compare the time and learning results of the two groups by completing the Subject Summary Data Sheet.

Suggested Procedure for Achieving the Experience Objectives

1. Read the directions for the experience.
2. Compare Program I to Program II and note the differences.
3. Complete Program II yourself. (Do not use a subject answer sheet, however.)
4. Conduct the experience with four subjects taking each program.
5. Score each program for each sheet.
6. Complete the Subject Summary Data Sheet.

Progress Chart

	Activity	Check each space when completed.

1. Read the directions for the experience _____
2. Compare Program I and II _____
3. Complete Program II yourself _____
4. Conduct experience with subject

     Program I: Subject 1 _____
                   Subject 2 _____
                   Subject 3 _____
                   Subject 4 _____

     Program II: Subject 1 _____
                    Subject 2 _____
                    Subject 3 _____
                    Subject 4 _____

5. Complete the Subject Summary Data Sheet _____

Directions for Conducting the Experience in Unit 9

Introduction: When preparing the actual instructional materials for a particular lesson, it is easy to overlook the use of concrete examples as a means of explaining generalized or abstract concepts. It is not unusual for a teacher who is preparing self-instructional material to state a series of "Ruls" and expect that a student will readily apply those rules to specific situations. That is the problem with the first set of instructional materials you will use in this experience. It is called "Dynamic Transpositional Inter-action Technique-I" and is basically a description of the rules used with the technique. (You should be aware that the technique was prepared especially for research and experience purposes; therefore, its major function is to provide a subject matter which people are not likely to have been exposed to previously.) In the second program, "Dynamic Transpositional Interaction Technique-II," examples have been added to help clarify the rules. You will give the first program to one group of four people and the second program to another different group of four people. You will measure the time it takes each individual to finish the assigned program and also measure the learning by means of the "Dynamic Transpositional Interaction Technique Test" which follows the programs. You will note that the tests for the two programs are identical, and that the programs differ only in that the second has examples which do not appear in the first.

Directions: Locate the subject in a place where he can work easily and not be disturbed. You should have either the Dynamic Transpositional Interaction Technique-I program or the Dynamic Transpositional Interaction Technique-II program, an answer sheet, and a pencil ready for the subject. You will need a pencil and clock to record the amount of time it takes the subject to finish the program *and the test.* Ask the subject to read the directions at the top of the program to himself while you read them aloud.

> This is a self-instructional program to help you learn a valuable strategy for explaining conversations between people. When you have completed this program, you will be able to analyze the interaction between any group of individuals and explain the dynamics of the conversation. Remember, the material on the next few pages will be instructional if you attempt to learn by yourself. You will be expected to respond by marking an X in the correct space *on your Answer Sheet.* Please do not write in the program. Do not turn a page until you have marked all of your choices. When you finish the program, go right on to the test. Are there any questions?

Try not to give any additional information when you answer questions. Most questions can be answered by simply rereading the appropriate directions. Enter the subject's total time (for both program and test) on the Subject Summary Data Sheet.

Subject Summary Data Sheet

Dynamic Transpositional Interaction Technique I

	Number Correct on Test	Time
Subject 1	_____	_____
Subject 2	_____	_____
Subject 3	_____	_____
Subject 4	_____	_____
SUM	_____	_____
MEAN*	_____	_____

Dynamic Transpositional Interaction Technique II

	Number Correct on Test	Time
Subject 1	_____	_____
Subject 2	_____	_____
Subject 3	_____	_____
Subject 4	_____	_____
SUM	_____	_____
MEAN*	_____	_____

* The MEAN is computed by dividing the SUM by the number of subjects in that group. For example if the four subjects got 15, 16, 13 and 18 items correct on the test, the SUM would be 15 + 16 + 13 + 18 = 62 and the MEAN would be 62 ÷ 4 = 15.5.

Dynamic Transpositional Interaction Technique I

This is a self-instructional program to help you learn a valuable strategy for explaining conversations between people. When you have completed this program, you will be able to analyze the interaction between any group of individuals and explain the dynamics of the conversation.

Remember, the material on the next few pages will be instructional if you attempt to learn *by yourself*. You will be expected to respond by marking an X in the correct space *on your Answer Sheet*. Please do not write in the program. Do not turn the page until you have marked all of your choices. When you finish the program, go right on to the test.

There are four concepts which are basic to the dynamic transpositional interaction theory. Let us begin by explaining what a *propositional* is. A propositional is a statement which suggests subsequent action on the part of either the communicator or the associate. (Do not be concerned at this time what the communicator or associate are.)

In each pair below, place an X by the statement which is a propositional:

> 1. _____A. "I didn't see them when I picked up the paper."
>
>   _____B. "You and I should go get the car right away."

> 2. _____A. "Who won the ball game today?"
>
>   _____B. "No one should go near that place next week."

A *responsive* is the second concept basic to the theory. A responsive is a statement immediately subsequent to a propositional which relates to the preceding propositional.

If the propositional was "Let's go home now," what would be a responsive in the pairs below. Place an X by the correct choice .

3. _____A. "Oh, is it time to leave?"

_____B. "Who owns the yellow chair?"

4. _____A. "I want to stop for some beer on the way."

_____B. "There isn't much choice in movies tonight."

The last two basic concepts are the *communicator* and the *associate*. The communicator is the person who produces the propositional. The associate is the person who produces the responsive.

Place an X by the communicator's statement below:

5. _____A. "Let's go get some coffee."

_____B. "O.K., wait for me, I'll get my coat."

Place an X by the associate's statement below:

6. _____A. "No one cares about people who fail except counselors . . . let's go see the counselor."

_____B. "O.K., when is he in his office?"

Non-positive interactionals are statements from either the communicator or the associate which are neither propositionals nor responsives.

Place an X by the non-positive interactionals in the pairs below:

7. _____A. "Boy, the sun is bright today."

_____B. "Let's go down to the gym before lunch."

8. _____A. "I really don't want to go with you to the store."

_____B. "The new chair fits very well with our Early American style."

Counter-propositionals are propositionals by the associate following one or more responsives, and subsequent to a propositional from the communicator.

Here is a part of another conversation:

Communicator—propositional: "Will you go to the show with me, tonight?"

Associate—responsive: "Sure, I need a break."

In the pairs below, place an X by the counter-propositional which could follow the partial conversation above:

9. _____A. Associate: "That great picture is playing."

_____B. Associate: "Let's go bar-hopping instead."

10. _____A. Associate: "But I'd rather visit the gallery, if you don't mind."

_____B. Associate: "And I'll take my sister along."

Upon making a counter-propositional, the associate becomes a counter-communicator.

In the pairs below, place an X by the counter-communicator.
Here is the start of the conversation:

> Person X: "Let's go sailing tomorrow afternoon."
> Person Y: "Well . . . okay, if we leave at 1:00."

---

11. _____A. Person Y: "Wait a minute, let's go hiking instead."

    _____B. Person Y: "Yeah, on second thought . . . sailing is fun."

---

12. _____A. Person Y: "Can you come with me to the museum instead?"

    _____B. Person Y: "Oh, nuts! at 1:00 I've got an appointment with my boss."

A *responsive-propositional* is a propositional by the associate which immediately follows a propositional from the communicator.

If the propositional was "Let's eat at Bill's," what would be a responsive-propositional in the pairs below?

Place an X by the correct choice.

---

13. _____A. "Bill's has bad hamburgers."

    _____B. "Let's go over to the Diner instead."

---

14. _____A. "No chance, man . . . let's eat cheap tonight."

    _____B. "Wow, would you look at that . . . ."

If a responsive-propositional occurs, then the person who made the responsive-propositional becomes the communicator.

In the pairs below, place an X by the person who is communicator by virtue of the fact that a responsive-propositional occurred, and if the initial propositional was "Let's go to the ball game."

---

15. _____A. "Not on your life! Let's go somewhere else where there isn't so much violence."

_____B. "Okay, but I need some money."

---

16. _____A. "What ball game?"

_____B. "How about the park instead?"

You have now completed the teaching part of this program. On the next few pages, you will find a test which you should do without the aid of the preceding pages.

FROM THIS POINT ON—DO NOT LOOK BACK TO PREVIOUS PAGES

Directions: On the left below are statements which make up part of a conversation. On the right below are multiple choice questions about the statements on the left. Answer each question by placing an X in the correct blank on your answer sheet.

Person A:

"Hi, I haven't seen you in a long time."

1. The statement on the left is a:

_____A. propositional
_____B. responsive
_____C. non-positive
_____D. counter-propositional

Person B:

"Hello, what a surprise to see you here."

2. The statement on the left is a:

_____A. propositional
_____B. responsive
_____C. non-positive interactional
_____D. counter-propositional

Person A:

"Let's get a drink somewhere and talk."

3. The statement on the left is a:

_____A. propositional
_____B. responsive
_____C. non-positive interactional
_____D. counter-propositional

Person B:

"Yeah, that would be fun."

4. The statement on the left was made by:

_____A. the communicator
_____B. the associate
_____C. the counter-communicator
_____D. none of the above

5. and it is a:

_____A. propositional
_____B. responsive
_____C. counter-propositional
_____D. responsive-propositional

Person A:

"Let's go to the League Bar."

6. The statement on the left is a:

    _____A. propositional
    _____B. responsive
    _____C. counter-propositional
    _____D. responsive-propositional

Person B:

"No, let's go to Joe's place."

7. The statement on the left is a:

    _____A. propositional
    _____B. responsive
    _____C. counter-propositional
    _____D. responsive-propositional

Person A:

"O.K., Joe's is fine."

8. The statement on the left was made by:

    _____A. the communicator
    _____B. the associate
    _____C. the counter-communicator
    _____D. none of the above

Person A:

"Wait a minute, on second thought . . . let's go to Seventh Street."

9. The statement at the left is a:

    _____A. propositional
    _____B. responsive
    _____C. counter-propositional
    _____D. responsive-propositional

Person B:

"O.K., whatever you want."

10. The statement at the left was made by:

    _____A. the communicator
    _____B. the associate
    _____C. counter-communicator
    _____D. none of the above

Here is another conversation.

Person C:

"I'm glad I met you here. I have something to discuss with you."

11. The statement at the left is a:

    _____A. propositional
    _____B. responsive
    _____C. counter-propositional
    _____D. non-positive interactional

Person D:

"Let's go to my place to talk."

12. The statement on the left is a:

    _____A. propositional
    _____B. responsive
    _____C. counter-propositional
    _____D. non-positive interactional

13. and was made by:

    _____A. communicator
    _____B. associate
    _____C. counter-communicator
    _____D. none of the above

Person C:

"O.K."

14. The statement on the left is a:

    _____A. propositional
    _____B. responsive
    _____C. counter-propositional
    _____D. none of the above

Person D:

"I've looked forward to seeing you."

15. The statement at the left is a:

    _____A. propositional
    _____B. responsive
    _____C. non-positive interactional
    _____D. none of the above

Person C:

"On second thought, let's go to a crowded bar."

16. The statement at the left is a:

    _____A. propositional
    _____B. counter-propositional
    _____C. responsive-propositional
    _____D. non-positive interactional

17. and was made by:

    _____A. the communicator
    _____B. the counter-communicator
    _____C. the associate
    _____D. none of the above

Person D:

"No, let's go to your place."

18. The statement on the left is a:

    _____A. propositional
    _____B. responsive
    _____C. responsive-propositional
    _____D. none of the above

Person C:

"Well, if that's what you
want, then O.K."

19. The statement at the left is a:

    _____A. responsive
    _____B. propositional
    _____C. counter-propositional
    _____D. none of the above

20. and was made by the:

    _____A. communicator
    _____B. counter-communicator
    _____C. associate
    _____D. none of the above

Subject Response Sheet

PROGRAM I

Name_____

Program	Test
1. _____	1. _____
2. _____	2. _____
3. _____	3. _____
4. _____	4. _____
5. _____	5. _____
6. _____	6. _____
7. _____	7. _____
8. _____	8. _____
9. _____	9. _____
10. _____	10. _____
11. _____	11. _____
12. _____	12. _____
13. _____	13. _____
14. _____	14. _____
15. _____	15. _____
16. _____	16. _____
	17. _____
	18. _____
	19. _____
	20. _____

Subject Response Sheet

PROGRAM I

Name _____

Program	*Test*
1. _____	1. _____
2. _____	2. _____
3. _____	3. _____
4. _____	4. _____
5. _____	5. _____
6. _____	6. _____
7. _____	7. _____
8. _____	8. _____
9. _____	9. _____
10. _____	10. _____
11. _____	11. _____
12. _____	12. _____
13. _____	13. _____
14. _____	14. _____
15. _____	15. _____
16. _____	16. _____
	17. _____
	18. _____
	19. _____
	20. _____

Subject Response Sheet
PROGRAM I

Name_____

Program	Test
1. _____	1. _____
2. _____	2. _____
3. _____	3. _____
4. _____	4. _____
5. _____	5. _____
6. _____	6. _____
7. _____	7. _____
8. _____	8. _____
9. _____	9. _____
10. _____	10. _____
11. _____	11. _____
12. _____	12. _____
13. _____	13. _____
14. _____	14. _____
15. _____	15. _____
16. _____	16. _____
	17. _____
	18. _____
	19. _____
	20. _____

Subject Response Sheet

PROGRAM I

Name_____

Program	Test
1. _____	1. _____
2. _____	2. _____
3. _____	3. _____
4. _____	4. _____
5. _____	5. _____
6. _____	6. _____
7. _____	7. _____
8. _____	8. _____
9. _____	9. _____
10. _____	10. _____
11. _____	11. _____
12. _____	12. _____
13. _____	13. _____
14. _____	14. _____
15. _____	15. _____
16. _____	16. _____
	17. _____
	18. _____
	19. _____
	20. _____

Dynamic Transpositional Interaction Technique II

This is a self-instructional program to help you learn a valuable strategy for explaining conversations between people. When you have completed this program, you will be able to analyze the interaction between any group of individuals, and explain the dynamics of the conversation.

Remember, the material on the next few pages will be instructional if you attempt to learn *by yourself*. You will be expected to respond by marking an X in the correct space *on your Answer Sheet*. Please do not write in the program. Do not turn a page until you have marked all of your choices. When you finish the program, go right on to the test.

There are four concepts which are basic to the dynamic transpositional interaction theory. Let us begin by explaining what a *propositional* is. A propositional is a statement which suggests subsequent action on the part of either the communicator or the associate. (Do not be concerned at this time what the communicator or associate are.)

An example of a propositional would be a statement such as this:

"Why don't we walk over to the library, and see if the book is there?"

In each pair below, place an X by the statement which is propositional:

1. _____A. "I didn't see them when I picked up the paper."	
_____B. "You and I should go get the car right away."	

2. _____A. "Who won the ball game today?"	
_____B. "No one should go near that place next week."	

A *responsive* is the second concept basic to the theory. A responsive is a statement immediately subsequent to a propositional which relates to the preceding propositional.

An example of a responsive would be a statement such as this:

If the propositional was "Why don't we go to the cafeteria?", the responsive would be "That's a great idea."

If the propositional was "Let's go home now," what would be a responsive in the pairs below. Place an X by the correct choice.

---

3. _____A. "Oh, is it time to leave?"

   _____B. "Who owns the yellow chair?"

---

4. _____A. "I want to stop for some beer on the way."

   _____B. "There isn't much choice in movies tonight."

The last two basic concepts are the *communicator* and the *associate*. The communicator is the person who produces the propositional. The associate is the person who produces the responsive.

An example of a communicator would be the person who says, "Come with me to the show."

An example of an associate would be the person who says, in response to the communicator, "O.K., I'd enjoy that."

Place an X by the communicator's statement below:

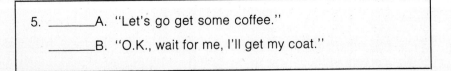

5. _____A. "Let's go get some coffee."

   _____B. "O.K., wait for me, I'll get my coat."

Place an X by the associate's statement below:

> 6. _____A. "No one cares about people who fail except coun-
> selors . . . let's go see the counselor."
>
> _____B. "O.K., when is he in his office?"

Non-positive interactionals are statements from either the communicator or the associate which are neither propositionals nor responsives.

An example of a non-positive interactional would be a statement such as this:

"Today is the second day in a row I've overslept."

Place an X by the non-positive interactionals in the pairs below:

> 7. _____A. "Boy, the sun is bright today."
>
> _____B. "Let's go down to the gym before lunch."

> 8. _____A. "I really don't want to go with you to the store."
>
> _____B. "The new chair fits very well with our Early American style."

Counter-propositionals are propositionals by the associate following one or more responsives, and subsequent to a propositional from the communicator. For example, suppose the following pattern occurred:

Communicator—propositional: "Let's get a Coke."
Associate—responsive: "O.K., I need a drink of something."
Associate—counter-propositional: "Let's get a beer instead."

Here is a part of another conversation:

Communicator—propositional: "Will you go to the show with me, tonight?"
Associate—responsive: "Sure, I need a break."

In the pairs below, place an X by the counter-propositional which could follow the partial conversation above:

---

9. _____A. Associate: "That great picture is playing."

_____B. Associate: "Let's go bar-hopping instead."

---

10. _____A. Associate: "But I'd rather visit the gallery, if you don't mind."

_____B. Associate: "And I'll take my sister along."

Upon making a counter-propositional, the associate becomes a counter-communicator.

For example, given that the propositional by the communicator was,

"Let's go for a drive."

and the responsive by the associate was,

"No, I've got things to do."

then if the next statement by the associate was,

"Let's study together at my place."

it would be a counter-propositional and the associate becomes the counter-communicator.

In the pairs below, place an X by the counter-communicator. Here is the start of the conversation:

Person X: "Let's go sailing tomorrow afternoon."
Person Y: "Well . . . okay, if we leave at 1:00."

---

11. _____A. Person Y: "Wait a minute, let's go hiking instead."

_____B. Person Y: "Yeah, on second thought . . . sailing is fun."

---

12. _____A. Person Y: "Can you come with me to the museum instead?"

_____B. Person Y: "Oh, nuts! at 1:00 I've got an appointment with my boss."

A *responsive-propositional* is a propositional by the associate which immediately follows a propositional from the communicator.

An example of a responsive-propositional would be a statement such as:

If the propositional was "Let's go home," the responsive-propositional would be "Let's go to Charlie's place instead."

If the propositional was "Let's eat at Bill's," what would be a responsive-propositional in the pairs below?

Place an X by the correct choice.

---

13. _____A. "Bill's has bad hamburgers."

_____B. "Let's go over to the Diner instead."

---

14. _____A. "No chance, man . . . let's eat cheap tonight."

_____B. "Wow, would you look at that . . ."

If a responsive-propositional occurs, then the person who made the responsive-propositional becomes the communicator. An example of a responsive-propositional made by the communicator would be a situation such as this:

Person A (who is the communicator initially because of the propositional which follows.) "Come with me to see the landlord."

Person B (who becomes the communicator initially because of the responsive-propositional with follows.) "No, you come with me to visit my uncle."

In the pairs below, place an X by the person who is communicator by virtue of the fact that a responsive-propositional occurred, and if the initial propositional was "Let's go to the ball game."

---

15. _____A. "Not on your life! Let's go somewhere else where there isn't so much violence."

_____B. "Okay, but I need some money."

---

16. _____A. "What ball game?"

_____B. "How about the park instead?"

You have now completed the teaching part of this program. On the next few pages, you will find a test which you should do without the aid of the preceding pages.

FROM THIS POINT ON—DO NOT LOOK BACK TO PREVIOUS PAGES

Directions: On the left below are statements which make up part of a conversation. On the right below are multiple choice questions about the statements on the left. Answer each question by placing an X in the correct blank on your answer sheet.

Person A:

"Hi, I haven't seen you in a long time."

1. The statement on the left is a:

_____A. propositional
_____B. responsive
_____C. non-positive
_____D. counter-propositional

Person B:

"Hello, what a surprise to see you here."

2. The statement on the left is a:

_____A. propositional
_____B. responsive
_____C. non-positive interactional
_____D. counter-propositional

Person A:

"Let's get a drink somewhere and talk."

3. The statement on the left is a:

_____A. propositional
_____B. responsive
_____C. non-positive interactional
_____D. counter-propositional

Person B:

"Yeah, that would be fun."

4. The statement on the left was

_____A. the communicator
_____B. the associate
_____C. the counter-communicator
_____D. none of the above

5. and it is a:

_____A. propositional
_____B. responsive
_____C. counter-propositional
_____D. responsive-propositional

Person A:

"Let's go to the League Bar."

6. The statement on the left is a:

_____A. propositional
_____B. responsive
_____C. counter-propositional
_____D. responsive-propositional

Person B:

"No, let's go to Joe's place."

7. The statement on the left is a:

_____A. propositional
_____B. responsive
_____C. counter-propositional
_____D. responsive-propositional

Person A:

"O.K., Joe's is fine."

8. The statement on the left was made by:

_____A. the communicator
_____B. the associate
_____C. the counter-communicator
_____D. none of the above

Person A:

"Wait a minute, on second thought . . . let's go to Seventh Street."

9. The statement at the left is a:

_____A. propositional
_____B. responsive
_____C. counter-propositional
_____D. responsive-propositional

Person B:

"O.K., whatever you want."

10. The statement at the left was made by:

_____A. the communicator
_____B. the associate
_____C. the counter-communicator
_____D. none of the above

Here is another conversation.

Person C:

"I'm glad I met you here. I have something to discuss with you."

11. The statement at the left is a:

_____A. propositional
_____B. responsive
_____C. counter-propositional
_____D. non-positive interactional

Person D:

"Let's go to my place to talk."

12. The statement on the left is a:

_____A. propositional
_____B. responsive
_____C. counter-propositional
_____D. non-positive interactional

13. and was made by:

_____A. communicator
_____B. associate
_____C. counter-communicator
_____D. none of the above

Person C:

"O.K."

14. The statement on the left is a:

_____A. propositional
_____B. responsive
_____C. counter-propositional
_____D. none of the above

Person D:

"I've looked forward to seeing you."

15. The statement at the left is a:

_____A. propositional
_____B. responsive
_____C. non-positive
_____D. none of the above

Person C:

"On second thought, let's go to a crowded bar."

16. The statement at the left is a:

_____A. propositional
_____B. counter-propositional
_____C. responsive-propositional
_____D. non-positive interactional

17. and was made by:

_____A. the communicator
_____B. the counter-communicator
_____C. the associate
_____D. none of the above

Person D:

"No, let's go to your place."

18. The statement on the left is a:

_____A. propositional
_____B. responsive
_____C. responsive-propositional
_____D. none of the above

Person C:

"Well, if that's what you
want, then O.K."

19. The statement at the left is a:

    _____A. responsive
    _____B. propositional
    _____C. counter-propositional
    _____D. none of the above

20. and was made by the:

    _____A. communicator
    _____B. counter-communicator
    _____C. associate
    _____D. none of the above

Subject Response Sheet

PROGRAM II

Name_____

Program   *Test*

1. _____   1. _____

2. _____   2. _____

3. _____   3. _____

4. _____   4. _____

5. _____   5. _____

6. _____   6. _____

7. _____   7. _____

8. _____   8. _____

9. _____   9. _____

10. _____   10. _____

11. _____   11. _____

12. _____   12. _____

13. _____   13. _____

14. _____   14. _____

15. _____   15. _____

16. _____   16. _____

                                        17. _____

                                        18. _____

                                        19. _____

                                        20. _____

Subject Response Sheet

PROGRAM II

Name_____

Program	Test
1. _____	1. _____
2. _____	2. _____
3. _____	3. _____
4. _____	4. _____
5. _____	5. _____
6. _____	6. _____
7. _____	7. _____
8. _____	8. _____
9. _____	9. _____
10. _____	10. _____
11. _____	11. _____
12. _____	12. _____
13. _____	13. _____
14. _____	14. _____
15. _____	15. _____
16. _____	16. _____
	17. _____
	18. _____
	19. _____
	20. _____

Subject Response Sheet

PROGRAM II

Name_____

Program

1. _____
2. _____
3. _____
4. _____
5. _____
6. _____
7. _____
8. _____
9. _____
10. _____
11. _____
12. _____
13. _____
14. _____
15. _____
16. _____

Test

1. _____
2. _____
3. _____
4. _____
5. _____
6. _____
7. _____
8. _____
9. _____
10. _____
11. _____
12. _____
13. _____
14. _____
15. _____
16. _____
17. _____
18. _____
19. _____
20. _____

Subject Response Sheet

PROGRAM II

Name_____

Program	Test
1. _____	1. _____
2. _____	2. _____
3. _____	3. _____
4. _____	4. _____
5. _____	5. _____
6. _____	6. _____
7. _____	7. _____
8. _____	8. _____
9. _____	9. _____
10. _____	10. _____
11. _____	11. _____
12. _____	12. _____
13. _____	13. _____
14. _____	14. _____
15. _____	15. _____
16. _____	16. _____
	17. _____
	18. _____
	19. _____
	20. _____

♦ SUMMARY

The purpose of this unit was to present a brief description of the programmed instruction approach to teaching and learning. The background portion of the unit explained the various phases associated with the methodology of programming instruction. The phases discussed were:

Phase 1. Specify the behavior to be learned.

Phase 2. Develop a way of measuring whether or not the behavior in 1 above was learned.

Phase 3. Develop an instructional procedure for teaching the behavior in 1 above.

Phase 4. Implement the instructional procedure and measurement in 2 and 3 above.

Phase 5. Revise the instructional procedure if the measurement instrument indicates the behavior was not learned.

The specific steps to be followed with each phase were outlined and examples of their application to teaching situations were given. Emphasis throughout the Background section of the unit was placed on the use of the individual phases, as well as the variety of media appropriate to programmed instruction.

The experience portion of the unit concentrated on Phases 4 and 5. Two sequences of programmed instruction were to be given to two different groups of subjects. The first sequence did not contain some components often essential to efficient and effective learning. The second sequence did contain those components and was considered to be the revised counterpart of the first sequence. The reader is encouraged to note the difference in rate of learning by measuring the amount of time required to finish the programs. In addition to time, learning was also measured by a test which was part of the programs and identical in each program. The outcome of the experience is predictable, but there are several questions which the reader should consider in light of the experience.

For instance, in more extensive research projects, the subjects seeing the programs with the examples not only learned more than the other subjects but also completed the programs in less time. This implies that they were actually learning faster when *more* material of a certain nature was present. Did you witness this with your subjects? Of course, with just four subjects in each group, there is a chance that you might see no differences or differences in the opposite direction from that expected. If this happened to you, you can probably appreciate why researchers use large groups of subjects and statistical procedures which account for chance differences.

Can you see the beneficial use of examples in other instructional media besides the paper and pencil program? in a lecture? in films? It is sometimes possible to employ only examples and aid the student in the derivation of the rules or the generalizations. Such strategy would be called "inductive" because of the progression from the concrete to the abstract, that is, from the examples to the rules. A "rule of thumb" the reader might wish to adopt and keep in mind is that whenever a deductive or inductive process is involved, examples should be plentiful in the instruction. There are, of course, situations in which induction and deduction are not necessary, for example when one must simply remember the Russian equivalent for an English word. How about your own subject matter specialty? What part do examples play in the learning or teaching of the information which you know best? In the examples presented in the Background portion of this unit, objectives were evident, but in both programs used in the experience there were no objectives stated. There was, however, a criterion test at the end of the programs. Can you state the objectives on the basis of that criterion test? One such objective could be, "Students will identify the propositional in a written conversation." As an exercise you might wish to state the other objectives illustrated by the test at the end of the program.

How could the criterion measure at the end of the program be different and be more effective as a measurement tool? Would the use of a tape recorder with a taped conversation improve the measure? Why? Compare the criterion measure in the program to criterion measures given in most classrooms. Of course, in most classrooms they are called "midterm" or "final exams." As another exercise you might wish to state objectives for some of the questions you have been given on midterm or final exams.

If you know the objectives for a program like those used in this experience, you can decide whether or not the criterion measure actually measures the objectives and whether or not the instructional procedure actually teaches the objectives. Did your four subjects meet the objectives as a result of the instruction in Dynamic Transpositional Interaction Technique II? If not, do you have any cues as to why not? What further revisions would you make? One way of approaching the answer to this question is to review the principles given in the Background information on instructional procedure preparation. Does the Dynamic Transpositional Interaction Technique II utilize all those principles stated?

How do you suppose the author of the programs analyzed the material and skills to be taught? Remember the Ruleg technique of analysis? Given the final product, i.e., the programs, it is pretty easy to hypothesize that rules were first generated for the Dynamic Transpositional Interaction

Technique, and at a later time the examples were developed. On the other hand, it is also possible to produce a flow chart illustrating the procedure of actually doing the technique. In attempting to do such a flow chart, you would first look at the conversation in the criterion measure and ask yourself, "What do I do first? Is it an action or a decision?" If a decision came first, you would have to follow both the "No" and the "Yes" choices until they either came back to the main flow or left the system altogether. If an action came first, it should be described and illustrated by the rectangular enclosure. Then, you move to the next step. Is it an action or a decision and so on? Which analysis method would seem to be most beneficial given the task to be learned? Consider a subject matter or skill that you know very well. Which analysis technique would seem to be most advantageous to you if you were to prepare a programmed sequence?

Getting back to the experience, how often did your subjects ask you whether or not their answers were correct? Did you get other indications that they would like to know what the correct answer was before proceeding to the next response? You will note that nowhere in Program I or II are there any answers to the questions given. In the early days of programmed instruction it was felt that answers, called confirmations, were absolutely necessary. Research data has since raised some serious doubts about the function of such confirmations. When a confirmation is given directly after the subject makes a response, the process is called "knowledge of results" and is thought to provide reinforcement for the response, thereby improving the learning. In some cases the learning has, indeed, been improved by knowledge of results, but in other cases no differences have been detected between programs with and without confirmations. A teacher should keep in mind the technique of providing immediate knowledge of results by giving confirmations to a student, but a hard and fast principle regarding their use cannot readily be stated. For the reader who is interested in further study of this question, a comparison of groups with and without knowledge of results is described in the Suggested Additional Activities.

The utilization of a programming methodology of instructional design will probably not be easily adopted by teachers in American classrooms. There are many long-standing practices which could inhibit the application of such a procedure, as well as, perhaps, provide a more functional method for getting the job done. There are, however, certain modifications and adaptations of the programming methodology which can be made by the individual teacher. Again, it is up to the individual to decide upon the usefulness, validity and desirability of any approach to learning and teaching. A psychologist cannot unequivocally say that this or that instruction design procedure is the "best."

There are a number of excellent books available in the area of instructional design, and they provide principles and strategies which can be of great use to the educator. If you wish to follow up on this important branch of educational psychology, you should consider the books and articles listed in the Suggested Additional Readings. For the reader who might like to experience firsthand some of the other problems and variables explored by psychological researchers, the Suggested Additional Activities offer several opportunities.

♦ SUGGESTED ADDITIONAL ACTIVITIES

1. In the portion of the Background material where instructional procedures are described, there is a principle which says that students should actively respond at regular intervals. What would happen to the learning of the Dynamic Transpositional Interaction Technique if regular responses were not called for? You might try typing up a list of the rules used in the technique. Give the list to a subject and simply ask him to learn these rules. Afterward give the subject(s) the same test used in the earlier experience. Compare the scores of the three groups, that is, the two groups in the earlier experience and this new group with just the rules. Note the approach of the subject when he is simply instructed to learn some verbal material. He might just memorize the rules without attempting to apply the rules to situations, which, of course, he would have to make up. On the other hand, your subjects might attempt to deductively reason out the examples of the rules rather than memorizing the verbal material present. What hypothesis would you favor? Do you think a group with just the rules and no necessity for active, regular responding will perform as well as the earlier groups which were given a chance to respond?

2. The Dynamic Transpositional Interaction Technique is a fairly complex set of operations, and sometimes requires several operational steps. Do you think younger children can learn to work with such a technique? High school sophomores? Eighth grade? Sixth grade? What problems would you expect to encounter as you use younger students as subjects? Would completion time increase? Which parts of the technique would younger children have difficulty with? Why? Is this true of most topics? How could you revise the instructional procedure (and retain the same criterion measure) so that it works for grade-school children? Try giving the programs to a cross section of elementary- and secondary-school students, and find out how they respond.

3. In the Summary section of this unit confirmations and knowledge of results were explained. Simply stated, knowledge of results is a process in which the subject is informed of the correctness of his response immediately after making the response. What effect would knowledge of results have on the performance of subjects in the Dynamic Transpositional Interaction Technique programs? You could gather some information to answer this question by writing the correct answer below each question in the programs. Have several subjects go through the programs with the correct answers present, and compare their learning scores with

the scores of the previous groups who did not have knowledge of results. You might find that knowledge of results will help alleviate some of the poor learning occurring when no examples were present, or you might not.

♦ SUGGESTED ADDITIONAL READINGS

For General Information About the Instructional Design Process

Anderson, R. C.; Faust, G. W.; Roderick, M. C.; Cunningham, D. J.; and Andre, T. *Current Research on Instruction*. Englewood Cliffs: Prentice-Hall, Inc., 1969.

Brethower, D. M.; Markle, D. G.; Rummler, G. A.; Schrader, A. W.; and Smith, D. E. P. *Programmed Learning: A Practicum*. Ann Arbor: Ann Arbor Publishers, 1964.

Coulson, J. E. *Programmed Learning and Computer-Based Instruction*. New York: John Wiley and Sons, Inc., 1961.

Glaser, R. *Investigations of the Characteristics of Programmed Learning Sequences*. Pittsburgh: University of Pittsburgh, 1961.

Gronlund, N. E. *Stating Behavioral Objectives for Classroom Instruction*. London: The Macmillan Company, 1970.

Kay, H.; Dodd, B.; and Sime, M. *Teaching Machines and Programmed Instruction*. Baltimore: Penguin Books, 1968.

Lumsdaine, A. A. *Teaching Machines and Programmed Learning*. Washington, D.C.: National Education Association, 1961.

Mager, R. F. *Preparing Objectives for Programming Instruction*. San Francisco: Fearon Press, 1962.

Markle, S. M. *Good Frames and Bad*. New York: John Wiley and Sons, Inc., 1969.

Merrill, D. M. *Instructional Design: Readings*. Englewood Cliffs: Prentice-Hall, 1971.

Smith, W. I., and Moore, J. W. *Programmed Learning*. Princeton: Van Nostrand, 1962.

For More Specific Information About Particular Aspects of Instructional Design

Anderson, R. C., and Faust, G. W. "The Effects of Strong Formal Prompts in Programmed Instruction." *American Educational Research Journal* 4(1967): 345–353.

Anderson, R. C.; Kulhavy, R. W.; and Andre, T. "Feedback Procedures in Programmed Instruction." *Journal of Educational Psychology* 62(1971):148–157.

Davis, R. H.; Marzocco, F. N.; and Denny, M. R. "Interaction of Individual Differences With Modes of Presenting Programmed Instruction." *Journal of Educational Psychology* 61(1970):198–205.

Holland, J. G. "A Quantitative Measure For Programmed Instruction." *American Educational Research Journal* 4(1967):87–103.

Hudson, W. W. "An Autotelic Teaching Experiment with Ancillary Casework Services." *American Educational Research Journal* 8(1971):467–485.

Johnson, R. "The Effect of Prompting, Practice and Feedback in Programmed Videotape." *American Educational Research Journal* 5(1968):73–81.

Oettinger, A., and Marks, S. "Educational Technology: New Myths and Old Realities." *Harvard Educational Review* 38(1968):697–717.

Payne, D. A.; Krathwohl, D. R.; and Gordon, J. "The Effect of Sequence on Programmed Instruction." *American Educational Research Journal* 4(1967): 125–133.

Shrable, K., and Sassenrath, J. M. "Effects of Achievement Motivation and Test Anxiety on Performance in Programmed Instruction." *American Educational Research Journal* 7(1970):219–221.